NEW DIRECTIONS FOR ADULT AND CONTINUING EDUCATION

Ralph G. Brockett, *University of Tennessee, Knoxville*
EDITOR-IN-CHIEF

Alan B. Knox, *University of Wisconsin, Madison*
CONSULTING EDITOR

# Professional Development for Educators of Adults

## Ralph G. Brockett
*University of Tennessee, Knoxville*

EDITOR

Number 51, Fall 1991

JOSSEY-BASS INC., PUBLISHERS, San Francisco

MAXWELL MACMILLAN INTERNATIONAL PUBLISHING GROUP
New York • Oxford • Singapore • Sydney • Toronto

PROFESSIONAL DEVELOPMENT FOR EDUCATORS OF ADULTS
*Ralph G. Brockett* (ed.)
New Directions for Adult and Continuing Education, no. 51
*Ralph G. Brockett,* Editor-in-Chief
*Alan B. Knox,* Consulting Editor

Microfilm copies of issues and articles are available in 16mm and 35mm,
as well as microfiche in 105mm, through University Microfilms Inc., 300
North Zeeb Road, Ann Arbor, Michigan 48106.

LC 85-644750          ISSN 0195-2242          ISBN 1-55542-765-0

NEW DIRECTIONS FOR ADULT AND CONTINUING EDUCATION is part of The
Jossey-Bass Higher and Adult Education Series and is published quarterly
by Jossey-Bass Inc., Publishers, 350 Sansome Street, San Francisco, California 94104-1310 (publication number USPS 493-930). Second-class post-
age paid at San Francisco, California, and at additional mailing offices.
POSTMASTER: Send address changes to New Directions for Adult and Continuing Education, Jossey-Bass Inc., Publishers, 350 Sansome Street, San
Francisco, California 94104-1310.

SUBSCRIPTIONS for 1991 cost $45.00 for individuals and $60.00 for institutions, agencies, and libraries.

EDITORIAL CORRESPONDENCE should be sent to the Editor-in-Chief,
Ralph G. Brockett, Dept. of Technological and Adult Education, University
of Tennessee, 402 Claxton Addition, Knoxville, Tennessee 37996-3400.

Cover photograph by Wernher Krutein/PHOTOVAULT © 1990.

Printed on acid-free paper in the United States of America.

# CONTENTS

# EDITOR'S NOTES

$A$s educators of adults, we are responsible for facilitating growth and development in the learners with whom we work. Yet we can easily overlook our own learning needs as professionals. In other words, we can forget to take care of ourselves.

Adult and continuing education is growing at a tremendous pace. Indeed, the field is very different from what it was even a decade ago. Thus, professional development has become much more than simply a matter of keeping up with the latest developments—it is now a basic responsibility that each of us has to our clients, our colleagues, our field, and ourselves. It is not enough merely to learn new techniques that can be incorporated uncritically into practice. Rather, each of us needs to be able to reflect on what it means to be an educator of adults and on how we choose to carry out this role.

The purpose of this volume is to explore a wide range of strategies for the process of professional development. A major assumption here is that effective leadership in adult and continuing education can be facilitated through an active professional development agenda. Bennis (1989, p. 139) cites a quotation from Apple chief executive officer John Sculley, who suggests that "leadership revolves around vision, ideas, direction, and has more to do with inspiring people as to direction and goals than with day-to-day implementation." Each of us, then, is a leader to the extent that we, as educators of adults, have a vision and seek to inspire others.

This volume has been developed with two specific audiences in mind. First, it is intended for those new to adult and continuing education, including beginning graduate students, who are seeking to learn about the scope of the field and trying to determine where they fit into it. Thus, this book can be a resource for both introductory-level graduate courses and staff development orientation sessions. Second, it is intended for those who are already practicing in the field but who are seeking new avenues for professional growth. For these readers, the book is especially designed to stimulate thinking about ways to make contributions to the field. Here, the book can be used either as a resource for self-directed professional development or as a guide for informal study and discussion groups.

The opening chapter sets the stage for the remainder of the volume by stressing that professional development is much more than merely accumulating a warehouse of new techniques that can be incorporated uncritically into practice. Rather, professional development is linked with professional artistry and revolves around helping the professional develop his or her unique style as an educator of adults.

Each of the next three chapters addresses the importance of the pro-

NEW DIRECTIONS FOR ADULT AND CONTINUING EDUCATION, no. 51, Fall 1991 © Jossey-Bass Inc., Publishers  1

fessional literature as a resource for professional development. Susan Imel, in Chapter Two, answers the question, "Where can I locate resources in adult and continuing education?" She discusses an array of information resources, such as data bases and clearinghouses, that can make the task more manageable.

In Chapter Three, the question shifts to "What do I do once I have located the resources?" Here, Harold W. Stubblefield provides suggestions on how to get more out of what one reads. Not only does he stress the value of current literature but he also offers some practical ideas on how to become familiar with many of the classic works in adult and continuing education.

Over the past two decades, the research base of adult and continuing education has grown tremendously, both in its quality and its quantity. There is much to be gained from this body of research. Thus, in Chapter Four, Elisabeth R. Hayes provides an introduction to the basic methods and procedures used by adult and continuing education researchers. The information in this chapter should help the reader who has a limited background in research design to become a more effective consumer of research.

Since this volume maintains that professional development involves not only accumulating new information and insights but also finding ways to contribute to the field, the next three chapters address vehicles through which such contributions can be made. In Chapter Five, Rodney D. Fulton discusses strategies new writers can use in order to get their ideas published. He describes several ways in which writers can focus their efforts, gain new understandings, and develop networks with other writers.

Although it would seem to go without saying that presentation skills are vital to success in adult education, little has been written on this topic. Joan E. Dominick, in Chapter Six, demystifies the process of making public presentations and offers some practical suggestions for making those presentations come alive.

Professional associations are another avenue through which educators of adults can simultaneously develop themselves and make contributions to the field. Drawing from their experiences in leadership roles, including that of president of a major professional association in adult and continuing education, Elaine Shelton and W. Franklin Spikes, in Chapter Seven, discuss ways in which associations can serve as an invaluable network for professional development and a means of making important contributions.

Ever since the first doctoral degrees in adult education were awarded in 1935, the importance of graduate study as a vehicle for professional development has increased steadily. Chapter Eight, by Catherine P. Zeph, offers a personal look at the graduate experience. The author shares insights with those readers who are seeking to get much more than just a degree from graduate study.

Critical reflection is central to the process of professional development. In Chapter Nine, John M. Peters presents a four-step process designed to help professionals improve their practice by critically reflecting on what they do and by gaining new insights from such reflection.

In Chapter Ten, I summarize the major themes from the previous chapters. In addition, I suggest ways to create a professional development plan designed to meet the individual practitioner's needs.

In closing, I would like to thank Martha Kreszock for her editorial assistance and Susan Flaherty for her help in preparing the final manuscript. Finally, I would like to thank the chapter authors, each of whom has helped to expand the possibilities for professional development.

Ralph G. Brockett
Editor

## Reference

Bennis, W. *On Becoming a Leader.* Reading, Mass.: Addison-Wesley, 1989.

*Ralph G. Brockett is associate professor of adult education at the University of Tennessee, Knoxville, and the editor-in-chief of New Directions for Adult and Continuing Education.*

*Professional development is vital to a vision for the future of adult and continuing education.*

# Professional Development, Artistry, and Style

*Ralph G. Brockett*

The field of adult and continuing education today struggles with a serious image problem. As Pittman (1989, p. 15) has noted, one of the major reasons for this is that "the great majority of people working in the field have never formed a close identification with it." The field's diversity is reflected in the myriad ways in which individuals enter the field, as well as in the multitude of settings where adult education takes place. Because most of us have entered adult education via some other field, our primary professional socialization has been in some other area, such as the behavioral sciences, teacher education, health professions, management, or human services. Until more adult and continuing educators come to view adult and continuing education as their primary field, we will continue to lack this sense of coherence or common identity.

One way to work toward a common identity is to emphasize an approach to professional development that is not limited solely to mastery of the skills one needs in order to perform effectively. Instead, this approach would emphasize that each of us needs to understand both the "big picture" of the field and how each of us can make a unique contribution to it. This chapter is designed to foster a view of professional development that stresses each person's unique abilities.

## Professionalization and Professional Development

Few issues have touched off more heated debate in adult and continuing education than the question of whether the field should strive toward increased professionalization. Because the notion of professional development implies that the field does comprise a "profession," we need to take a brief look at this issue here. Nearly three decades ago, Cotton (1964) pointed out that the adult education movement grew out of two traditions. The first of these, the social reform tradition, emerged in the 1920s. It held that adult education should be seen as a vehicle for challenging and changing inequities in the existing social order. Early proponents of this viewpoint in the United States included Eduard C. Lindeman, Joseph K. Hart, Charles A. Beard, and Alexander Meiklejohn. The professional tradition emerged in the 1930s, at least partially as a reaction to the perceived "utopianism" (but not necessarily to the social concern) of social reform. The professional tradition's emphasis on developing an adult education "movement" coincided with the development of the first graduate programs in adult education in the United States and was advocated early on by such individuals as Lyman Bryson, Alvin Johnson, E. L. Thorndike, Everett Dean Martin, and Morse A. Cartwright. Cotton (1964) argued that each of these traditions has much to offer contemporary adult education. Yet, today, it seems that the distance between these two traditions is still great, perhaps even greater than in the past. The distance becomes readily apparent when reading a recent New Directions for Adult and Continuing Education volume (Quigley, 1989) that explores the degree to which the field has actually fulfilled its promise.

In looking at the issue from an historical-philosophical perspective, Carlson (1977, p. 56) argued that increased emphasis on professionalization has diminished one of the hallmarks on which the field was based—the notion of "friends educating each other." He suggested that two deleterious by-products of professionalization are an overemphasis on "schooling" rather than education and efforts to establish certification for adult educators. More recently, Collins (1990, p. 3) has argued that emphasis on professionalization will not lead to such goals as "competent performance" and "more secure jobs in adult education."

While I agree that the concerns raised by critics of professionalization are legitimate, I believe that until adult and continuing education can stake out its own place as a profession respected and recognized by the larger society, we will continue to function on the fringes, with little real influence on the issues affecting society at large. For me, then, the question is not "Should adult and continuing education professionalize?" but rather, "What kind of a profession should we strive to be?"

I believe it is possible for adult and continuing education to increase its visibility and credibility in society without destroying the vitality and spontaneity of "friends helping educate friends." For instance, Cervero (1985) has suggested that four key elements of adult education conflict with the traditional model of professionalization. These contradictions are as follows:

1. Unlike professions where the client is in a "subordinate position" and thus cannot understand one's own needs, much (actually most) adult learning activity takes place without an adult educator.

2. The interaction between adult educator and learner is characterized by mutual involvement in the planning process, while decision making in more traditional professions typically lies in the hands of the professional.

3. While most traditional professions offer credentials to their members through "standardized testing of cognitive knowledge such as in licensing and certification examinations" (Cervero, 1985, 14), such an approach is not likely to be useful in assessing the skills needed in working with adult learners.

4. Adult and continuing educators strive to take a holistic view of the learners with whom they work, while those in traditional professions are typically concerned only with those aspects of the client that fall within their area of specialization.

Cervero suggests that it is possible to create an alternative vision of professionalization that stresses active learner involvement in the planning process and that uses a human rights model emphasizing that individuals have a "right to know" (p. 15) rather than a medical model where learning needs are likely to be viewed as deficiencies. This perspective recognizes that much successful adult learning takes place without the intervention of a professional and that such intervention can sometimes be detrimental; it also acknowledges that individuals and their learning needs cannot be isolated from the social, political, and economic environment in which they arise and that the relationship between adult learners and educators of adults is symbiotic—in other words, "while they would probably survive without us, we could not exist without them" (Cervero, 1985, p. 15). Finally, this view of professionalization emphasizes that educators of adults are not "value-neutral" but rather are "political actors within a social structure" (p. 16) in programs designed either to promote change or to preserve the status quo.

The point to be made here is that it is not professionalization itself that threatens the field. Rather, it is a vision of professionalization that stresses such values as client dependence, professional authority, and rigidly defined criteria for the right to practice that has led many to be skeptical of adult education as a profession. It is my belief that professionalization is a desirable and even essential goal if adult and continuing education is to have a major impact on society in the coming century. In addition, I believe that it is crucial for us to create a professional vision that truly characterizes the strengths of our own field, rather than to follow blindly some existing model, such as that found in social work, law, or the health professions. The ideas presented in this chapter and, indeed, in the chapters that follow are largely based on such a vision.

## Artistry in Professional Development

Professional practice can be viewed as an art. Schön (1987) uses the term *professional artistry* to describe "the kinds of competence practitioners sometimes display in unique, uncertain, and conflicted situations of practice" (p. 22). Schön suggests that such artistry takes place through the process of "reflection-in-action," where once a person has learned how to do something, it is possible to "execute smooth sequences of activity, recognition, decision, and adjustment without having . . . to 'think about it' " (p. 26). In other words, professional artistry takes place when one is able to practice in a spontaneous way, without having to think through the problem-solving process for each specific situation. Each of us acquires this artistry as we develop the ability to reflect on our practice and as we incorporate this reflection into our tacit knowledge base. It is this knowledge base that allows us to recognize something immediately without consciously going through the process of recognition, just as we recognize a familiar face in a crowd or a familiar song on the radio.

In my own thinking about professional development, I have drawn on Schön's view, but I use a slightly different description of artistry. To me, the two essential elements of artistry are technique and style. Technique essentially encompasses the skills needed to perform a task. Thus, it consists of the nuts-and-bolts abilities that are prerequisite to successful practice. Some examples of technique might include being able to write objectives, knowing how to develop brochures and other marketing tools, being able to develop and manage a budget, being able to use different teaching techniques, or knowing how to evaluate outcomes.

To be sure, techniques such as these are essential to successful practice in adult and continuing education. But training and in-service programs, as well as instructional materials, frequently stop at this level. Indeed, educators themselves often seek out only the information that is related strictly to technique. "Just tell me what I need to know to do my job"—or the more popular "just the facts"—is the battle cry of such individuals. In the 1960s, Cotton (1964) confronted this attitude by stating that "adult educators should accept their responsibility to be something more than program technicians. . . . The unfortunate fact is that there are too many program technicians and not enough adult educators (in the true meaning of that term)" (p. 86). Basing his ideas on an analysis of the historical literature of adult and continuing education, he goes on to make the following recommendation: "We, as adult educators, must do those things that have to be done to make adult education socially significant. In other words, the degree to which the potential of adult education is realized depends upon our dedication, commitment, and intellectual vigor—upon the extent to which we fulfill our roles as adult educators" (p. 87).

Dedication, commitment, intellectual vigor—these are all elements that go beyond technical competence. And this is the point I wish to stress. Technique is necessary for successful practice, but it is not enough! The educator who limits his or her own continuing education to the mere mastery, in an uncritical way, of new techniques is doomed to perpetuate the kind of adult education that Cotton decries.

There is much more to successful practice than mastery of techniques, and it is the notion of artistry that offers insight here. Style is what allows us to make distinctions—often tacitly—among individuals who share a particular knowledge or skill. In contemporary music, for example, what distinguishes Jimi Hendrix from Eric Clapton or Miles Davis from Wynton Marsalis is not technical skill as a musician but style—the elusive quality that lets the listener recognize a particular sound as belonging to a particular individual. This is equally true of comparisons among writers, painters, actors, or any other type of artist. In any form of art, one must possess a certain level of technical skill in order to succeed. But skill alone is not enough. It is style that allows the artist to breathe life into the art form, making it possible to leave his or her distinct imprint.

Just as style is important to the successful artist, so, too, is it of value to the educator of adults who strives for distinction. But the kind of style being discussed here is not something that can be easily classified. Style manifests itself in how one expresses oneself, which in turn is typically linked to such characteristics as personality, basic value system, and previous life experience. Thus, a person who believes that human nature is basically good and that adult and continuing education can serve as a vehicle for personal growth will come across somewhat differently from the person who believes that human nature is shaped by the environment and thus emphasizes a behavioristic, competency-based approach to the education of adults. Similarly, the person who is able to make his or her greatest contribution by working as a tutor helping individuals learn to read projects a different style from a professor whose major contributions come in the form of published research investigations. The point here is not to place relative value on these different approaches; rather, it is to show that there is virtually an unlimited number of ways in which to make a special contribution to the field. Our task, as educators of adults, is to determine how each of us can contribute in a way that is consistent with our unique abilities, interests, and aspirations. That, in essence, is what style is about.

## Cultivating Style: Some Ingredients to Consider

If we accept the premise that style is a crucial element of successful practice, then we can begin to explore how to develop it. While style is elusive and cannot easily be prescribed, I believe there are several basic ingredients that can be acquired through professional development activities and that allow an individual style to emerge. Three such components include the development of a professional sense of self, the making of a basic commitment to the field of adult and continuing education, and the discovery of and ability to act on one's unique abilities.

**Developing a Professional Sense of Self.** One of the most basic ingredients of style is one's sense of self. Each of us has come to the practice and study of adult and continuing education with a wide range of experiences, and whether we realize it or not, these experiences play an important role in how we view the field and in how we carry out our responsibilities as educators. In developing a professional style, we must be aware of the basic values we bring with us into our practice. In other words, we need to understand our "working philosophy" of adult and continuing education (Apps, 1973).

One technique that facilitates the development of this professional sense of self is to articulate one's philosophy of adult and continuing education. This is an activity that I regularly use in one of my graduate courses. Over the years, students have consistently remarked that this is one of the most difficult activities in the course, for it forces them to look inward to understand not just what they believe but why they believe what they do; at the same time, these individuals remark that writing such a statement is one of the most rewarding activities of the course. Hiemstra (1988) describes a practical process for developing a statement of personal philosophy, and Apps (1985) presents a more detailed process for improving practice through systematic analysis.

Another ability that is essential to the development of a sense of self is critical reflection. This process is described in Chapter Nine in this volume. Here we need only emphasize that self-reflection is a core element in developing one's style.

Still another factor is the ability to incorporate all of one's life experiences into one's professional style. One's professional sense of self is not something that can be turned on and off like a light switch. Rather, what we bring to our professional role includes much of who we are outside this role. For example, I often refer in my teaching to popular music, film, or literature in order to illustrate certain points I am trying to make. Another personal interest that I draw on in my work is the reading of biographies; these help me to gain insight into both the joys and struggles of individuals who have been successful in spite of obstacles. Developing a style involves letting some of our "other" selves spill over into our "professional" selves; this is a valuable process as long as we are careful not to try to persuade or pressure others into adopting our own positions.

**Making a Commitment to the Field.** A second ingredient that can contribute to the development of a professional style is the process of identifying ourselves with the adult and continuing education field. This commitment involves an ongoing process of professional socialization. In law schools, the phrase "learning to love the law" (Turow, 1977, p. 35) is sometimes heard, especially among beginning law students. Essentially, this is the process through which students become so immersed in the study of law that they begin to be able to "think like a lawyer." While adult and continuing education is different from the legal profession and the training for these two groups also differs greatly, this line of thinking can still be useful within our own field. Like any other professional group, educators of adults need to be able to understand, appreciate, and take pride in their field and its basic concepts, theories, historical underpinnings, and resources.

Griffith (1989) made the following distinction between educators of adults and adult educators: "Educators of adults have focused goals that typically address pressing problems in a single sector of the field of adult education, while adult educators have broad aspirations for the entire field" (p. 5). This distinction is an important one, although I describe it in a slightly different way. My distinction is between "adult educators" and those who "do" adult education. Here, the former group consists of those who identify themselves primarily as members of the adult and continuing education field, while the latter group is comprised of individuals (such as nurses, librarians, social workers, military personnel, and clergy) who identify primarily with other professions but whose responsibilities often involve direct practice with adult learners.

The value of this distinction lies in its ability to quell a major criticism of professionalization in adult education, which warns of the potential for an elitist hierarchy within the field. Instead, this distinction can make the issue of elitism moot, since it makes no attempt to compare or rank the different categories. One does not need to be a professional social worker in order to assist others in meeting certain social needs; however, such a person does not claim to *be* a social worker. Nor does one need to be a professional in order to share financial advice with another individual, as long as the adviser does not claim to be a "professional" financial consultant. The same is true for adult education. One obviously does not need a graduate degree in adult education to teach a personal interest course to a group of adults, and such teachers, without claiming to be "professional" adult educators, play an important role. On the other hand, if we are to have a truly viable profession of adult and continuing education, we do need to have some individuals who identify themselves as professionals and who engage in a professional socialization process. My point is that *both* groups are valuable to adult learners; devoting time and energy to determining which group is "more important" is rather like trying to prove that apples are better than oranges.

**Finding One's Own Voice.** This final component is actually a synthesis or result of the previous ones. The central question here is "How do I want to present myself as an adult and continuing education professional?"

The notion of professional style recognizes that each person possesses a unique combination of abilities. Finding one's voice means making decisions about how one wants to contribute to the field. For some, this means being good at planning programs. Others may find their voice in a social activist role. Still others will find that they can make their greatest contribution by publishing and being active in professional associations. Such decisions can only emerge when one takes a serious look at the full range of possibilities open to him or her. Bennis (1989, p. 123), in suggesting that as leaders we need to "strike hard, try everything," asks, "How can *you* best express you?" This sums up the process of finding one's voice.

## Conclusion

Each of us has something special to contribute to the education of adults. One way of thinking about professional development is as a vehicle that will help each of us to find the best way to make this contribution. Often, discussions of professional development for adult and continuing educators tend to revolve around solving problems related to immediate concerns in a specific practice setting. This is certainly a legitimate aspect of professional development, but the person who is able to look beyond such immediate concerns is in a much stronger position to make a lasting contribution to the education of adults. Successful professional development in adult and continuing education is most likely to occur when there is a balance between emphasis on techniques for effective practice and opportunities to help educators cultivate their own unique professional style. The following chapters, then, challenge us to explore areas of professional development that may be unfamiliar or to look at familiar areas in new ways. As such, each chapter contributes to the reader's exploration of personal style.

## References

Apps, J. W. *Toward a Working Philosophy of Adult Education.* Syracuse, N.Y.: Syracuse University Publications in Continuing Education, 1973.

Apps, J. W. *Improving Practice in Continuing Education: Modern Approaches for Understanding the Field and Determining Priorities.* San Francisco: Jossey-Bass, 1985.

Bennis, W. *On Becoming a Leader.* Reading, Mass.: Addison-Wesley, 1989.

Carlson, R. A. "Professionalization of Adult Education: An Historical-Philosophical Analysis." *Adult Education,* 1977, *28* (1), 53–63.

Cervero, R. M. "The Predicament of Professionalism for Adult Education." *Adult Literacy and Basic Education,* 1985, *9* (1), 11–17.

Collins, M. "Some Observations on the Role of the Commission of Professors." In A. Blunt (ed.), *Proceedings of the 1990 Annual Conference of the Commission of Professors of Adult Education.* Saskatoon, Saskatchewan: College of Education, University of Saskatchewan, 1990.

Cotton, W. E. "The Challenge Confronting American Adult Education." *Adult Education,* 1964, *14* (2), 80–88.

Griffith, W. S. "Has Adult and Continuing Education Fulfilled Its Early Promise?" In B. A. Quigley (ed.), *Fulfilling the Promise of Adult and Continuing Education*. New Directions for Adult and Continuing Education, no. 44. San Francisco: Jossey-Bass, 1989.

Hiemstra, R. "Translating Personal Values and Philosophy into Practical Action." In R. G. Brockett (ed.), *Ethical Issues in Adult Education*. New York: Teachers College Press, 1988.

Pittman, V. "What Is the Image of the Field Today?" In B. A. Quigley (ed.), *Fulfilling the Promise of Adult and Continuing Education*. New Directions for Adult and Continuing Education, no. 44. San Francisco: Jossey-Bass, 1989.

Quigley, B. A. (ed.). *Fulfilling the Promise of Adult and Continuing Education*. New Directions for Adult and Continuing Education, no. 44. San Francisco: Jossey-Bass, 1989.

Schön, D. A. *Educating the Reflective Practitioner: Toward a New Design for Teaching and Learning in the Professions*. San Francisco: Jossey-Bass, 1987.

Turow, S. *One L: An Inside Account of Life in the First Year at Harvard Law School*. New York: Putnam, 1977.

*Ralph G. Brockett is associate professor of adult education at the University of Tennessee, Knoxville.*

*The ability to identify, access, select, and use information resources
is essential for ongoing professional development in adult and
continuing education.*

# Information Resources for Professional Development

*Susan Imel*

Keeping up with advancements in the professional literature is an important
aspect of professional development in any field. The rapid growth of a field's
literature and ongoing changes in the way information is made available
make staying current with the literature a challenging task. Although changes
in technology have resulted in more rapid production and faster transmission of information, the rate of comprehending information—about three
hundred words per minute—has remained relatively constant (Becker,
1986). One manifestation of the information explosion is what Wurman
(1989) terms *information anxiety:* the state of being surrounded by vast
amounts of information—but information that does not provide the required
knowledge. According to Wurman, the following situations are likely to produce information anxiety: not understanding information, feeling over-
whelmed by the amount of information to be understood, not knowing if
certain information exists, not knowing where to find information, and knowing exactly where to find information but not having the key to access it.

The task of keeping up with the professional literature in adult education may create information anxiety. Rapid expansion of the field's literature base makes it difficult to keep abreast of the latest publications as well
as to evaluate their relevance to any ongoing work. What little time most
adult and continuing educators have for discretionary reading must be
used wisely.

Therefore, the ability to identify, access, select, and use information
resources is essential for continuing professional development, as these
processes can help individuals make more effective use of the literature.
Those who understand how to access such information sources as elec-

NEW DIRECTIONS FOR ADULT AND CONTINUING EDUCATION, no. 51, Fall 1991 © Jossey-Bass Inc., Publishers

tronic data bases have a distinct advantage over those who do not. However, unless these individuals also know how to select the most appropriate resources, they, too, will be at a disadvantage. Dealing with information overload requires an awareness of the wide range of possible resources as well as the ability to sort through and evaluate their relevance (Imel, 1990).

This chapter provides some strategies for staying current with the information resources in adult education. First, it describes the types and sources of available resources; then, some approaches for making intelligent choices from among this range of resources are presented.

## Types of Information Resources

Adult education information appears in a variety of formats, with the most common print sources being books, periodicals, dissertations, and fugitive materials (Imel, 1989). Although more nonprint adult education information resources, including audiotapes, videotapes, and microcomputer software, are now available, they will not be discussed here.

**Books.** Books are a primary source of information about adult education. Because they are durable and because libraries have systematic procedures for collecting and classifying them, much of the literature of adult education is available in this format. Due to their specialized nature, however, books about adult education generally can only be acquired at large public or university libraries. Because many books considered to be classics are now out of print, they are not obtainable (Imel, 1989). Fortunately, two of the adult education classics—Lindeman's ([1926] 1989) *The Meaning of Adult Education* and Houle's ([1961] 1988) *The Inquiring Mind*—have been reprinted by the Oklahoma Research Center for Continuing Professional and Higher Education. Individuals can stay current with new book publications by reading book review sections of professional journals and asking to be placed on publishers' mailing lists. Stubblefield takes a closer look at adult education books in Chapter Three.

**Periodicals.** Periodicals, including journals and newsletters, are an important adult education resource. The number of journals and newsletters devoted to adult and continuing education has increased as the field has grown. Also, many articles about aspects of adult education frequently appear in nonadult education journals. Examples of adult education journals include *Adult Education Quarterly* and *Adult Learning*, which have a general focus on North American adult education; *Convergence* and the *International Journal of Lifelong Education*, which focus on international adult education; the *Journal of Extension*, the *Training and Development Journal*, and the *Journal of Continuing Higher Education*, all of which are intended for specific audiences within the field; and the *Journal of Adult Education*, published by the Mountain Plains Adult Education Association, which has a regional focus.

Although adult educators may have access to some current periodical literature through personal subscriptions, institutional libraries, or resource centers, a comprehensive range of adult education periodical literature is usually available only in large university libraries (Imel, 1989). Information about specific articles can be obtained by searching such data bases as Social SciSearch or that maintained by the Educational Resources Information Center (ERIC).

**Dissertations.** Dissertations are also a source of information on adult education. More than three thousand doctoral degrees have been awarded in adult education (Long, 1987), and the dissertations that have been written to fulfill the degree requirements can be accessed through *Dissertations Abstracts International.*

**Fugitive Materials.** Many resources in adult education are classified as "fugitive" because their availability is not well known or publicized or because they may be difficult to acquire. Fugitive materials include items such as conference papers and proceedings, research studies, reports of government-funded projects, and monographs. Despite their ephemeral nature, many fugitive materials have made an important contribution to the knowledge base of adult education, and ERIC has been instrumental in making them much more accessible (Imel, 1989).

## Sources of Information Resources

Information resources in adult education are diverse and scattered. There are, however, three major types of access to these resources: libraries, information data bases, and clearinghouses or resource centers. Becoming knowledgeable about these sources will help one keep abreast of the literature.

**Libraries.** Libraries are a primary source of information in adult education, especially books and journals. College and university libraries at institutions where graduate programs in adult and continuing education are located are particularly good sources of adult education information. However, through the auspices of interlibrary loan programs, the resources of these libraries are available to individuals at other locations. Some state libraries have good collections of adult education literature. Although local libraries may not have specialized books or journals in adult education, most provide access to information data bases. Individuals can inquire at their local libraries about the availability of specific resources as well as about accessing the resources of collections at other libraries.

There are several outstanding collections of adult education literature in university libraries within the United States, but the Adult and Continuing Education Research Collection at Syracuse University is particularly significant. Generally regarded as the largest English-language adult and continuing education archives in the world, the collection contains papers from about twenty organizations and thirty-five individuals. Under the auspices of the Syracuse University Kellogg Project, an information system is being developed that will give individuals immediate access to information in the collection (*Kellogg Project Overview*, 1990).

**Information Data Bases.** Information data bases store collections of related information that can be retrieved via computer using information retrieval software. When stored, the materials have usually been indexed or classified using a vocabulary control device—for example, a thesaurus, a list of subject headings, or some other specialized classification scheme. This controlled vocabulary is used to retrieve information from a data base (Niemi and Imel, 1987).

Some information data bases are also available in CD-ROM format. CD-ROM, which stands for compact disk–read-only memory, is a technology with a high storage capacity; thus, it is an appropriate delivery medium for large collections of information or data bases (McLaughlin, 1987). Retrieving information from CD-ROM versions of data bases is similar to on-line searching.

There are a number of data bases that contain information related to the field of adult education. Two comprehensive references that can be used to select the most appropriate data base are the *Encyclopedia of Information Systems and Services* (1990) and *Datapro Directory of On-Line Services* (1990). Catalogues from data-base vendors—companies that provide on-line access to a number of information data bases—can also be used to choose data bases. Some information data bases that are particularly good sources of adult education resources are mentioned here. (Except where noted, *BRS Information Technologies 1990 Database Catalog*, 1990, and *DIALOG Database Catalog 1990* are the sources of information about the data bases described.)

*ERIC.* This resource is considered to be the primary information data base for adult education materials, due to its purpose and to its history of service to the field. Currently funded by the U.S. Department of Education's Office of Educational Research and Improvement, ERIC is designed to put the results of educational research and practice into the hands of educational researchers, practitioners, policy makers, and others interested in such information. Since 1966, ERIC has been collecting and classifying all types of educational materials and focusing on fugitive ones. ERIC also contains information about journal literature. More than seven hundred education-related journals, including all major adult education journals published both in the United States and abroad, are scanned regularly, and articles are selected for inclusion in the data base (Imel, 1989; Niemi and Imel, 1987).

Since 1966, more than fourteen thousand items whose major topic is related to adult education have been selected for inclusion in ERIC. Some examples of the materials found in ERIC include papers and proceedings from adult and continuing education conferences, such as the Adult Education Research Conference, American Association for Adult and Continuing Education Annual Conference, and Midwest Research-to-Practice Conference in Adult and Continuing Education; reports of projects funded through Section 353 (formerly 310) of the Adult Education Act; government-funded research reports related to adult education; and policy papers produced by professional associations and private agencies.

In the past, professional searchers handled access to ERIC. However, the availability of microcomputers and the packaging of the ERIC data base in CD-ROM format have made ERIC more accessible to the general public. Many individuals now choose to access ERIC without the assistance of a professional searcher. A subject search of ERIC results in bibliographical information plus an abstract of all information in the ERIC data base on the topic. Because ERIC is a document retrieval data base, most documents (the so-called fugitive literature) are available on either microfiche or paper from the ERIC Document Reproduction Service. However, journal articles must be obtained through other sources such as libraries, resource centers, or journal reprint services (Imel, 1989).

*Dissertation Abstracts Online (DAO).* This resource provides on-line access to the same information about dissertations on adult education topics that appears in the print index *Dissertation Abstracts International.* Although abstracts are only included for those dissertations completed since 1980, most dissertations accepted at an accredited institution since 1861 are indexed by subject, title, and author. Since 1988, DAO has included British and European dissertations and master's abstracts. Useful in determining trends in research, DAO is most commonly used to verify original research.

*AgeLine.* Adult educators seeking information about older adults may want to consult AgeLine, a data base produced jointly by the American Association of Retired Persons and the National Gerontology Resource Center. Covering 1978 to the present, its more than twenty-eight thousand records include bibliographical citations and an original abstract. Approximately two-thirds of the data base consists of journal citations, with the balance representing books, book chapters, and reports. Unlike ERIC and DAO, there is no print equivalent of AgeLine.

*British Education Index (BEI).* This resource includes information on significant journal literature relating to education and thesis literature and covers all aspects and fields of education from preschool to adult and higher education. A search of BEI results in bibliographical references retrieved using subject descriptions.

*ABI/Inform.* This major source of journal literature covering areas of interest to the business community may interest adult educators concerned with human resource development. Approximately eight hundred primary publications in business and related fields are currently scanned for inclusion in ABI/Inform.

*Social SciSearch.* Because it enables the user to trace research results both forward and backward in time, Social SciSearch (SSCI) is an important research tool for professionals and students in the social and behavioral sciences, including adult education. It indexes every significant item from 1,500 of the most important social sciences journals. In addition to providing conventional retrieval through title words, source authors, journal names, corporate sources, and so forth, SSCI also provides for retrieval through an author's cited references.

Other information data bases with which adult educators may wish to become familiar include Religion Index, Sociological Abstracts, PsycINFO (formerly *Psychological Abstracts*), Vocational Education Curriculum Materials, and National Technical Information Service (NTIS) Bibliographic Database. Although professional searchers are able to make suggestions about appropriate information data bases, familiarity with the relevant names facilitates staying current with resources.

**Clearinghouses and Resource Centers.** Several clearinghouses and resource centers disseminate information about adult education to a variety of audiences, including administrators, teachers, researchers, students, and the general public. Some of these organizations are national in scope, while others are state-level organizations. Functions provided by clearinghouses and resource centers include searching information data bases, providing information about resources, maintaining collections of materials, and offering referrals to other agencies and organizations serving adult learners. Many also develop and make available newsletters as well as free and inexpensive materials related to adult education resources (Imel, 1990). Information about clearinghouses and resource centers serving adult educators can be found in the following directories: *Directory of National Clearinghouses: Resource Centers and Clearinghouses Serving Adult Educators and Learners* (Clearinghouse on Adult Education and Literacy, 1990) and *Adult Education State Resource and Information Centers* (Adult Learning and Literacy Clearinghouse, 1990).

## Strategies for Identifying Resources

Knowledge about the types of resources that are available and where they are located is one piece of the information puzzle, but this awareness is best used in combination with some other strategies to help identify the most appropriate resources. Relevant questions include the following (Imel, 1990): What type of information is sought? For what purpose or purposes will it be used? How much information is needed? How much is already known about the topic? What resources are available to be devoted to the task? How will the information be used? Who can assist in selecting the best strategies to begin an information search? The strategies used to identify resources for a research project will be different than those that help a practitioner acquire an overview of a topic. The former might involve inquiries to a number of sources, while the latter might be as simple as identifying and locating a good review article on the subject.

Common strategies used to locate sources of information include scanning references in related publications, such as books and journal articles; communicating with others; and searching information data bases (Cooper, n.d.). Using lists of references in publications is an excellent way to locate additional information on a topic. Sometimes one book or article can lead to an entire body of related information. Closely associated with this strategy is the approach of browsing through journals and newsletters for announcements or reviews of new publications. New books in adult and continuing education are regularly announced in the *Chronicle of Higher Education*'s column, "New Books in Higher Education."

Sometimes the best way to locate information is through personal contact. This strategy may include informal conversations in which information is obtained serendipitously as well as more deliberate contact with those who are working in a particular area. Personal contacts can be particularly helpful if little or nothing is known about the topic. Most adult educators are more than happy to share information about their work, including key information sources. Adult education resource center and clearinghouse personnel are frequently able to identify information sources. These individuals work with adult education information resources on a daily basis and are knowledgeable about new materials, and they are usually able to make referrals to other sources of information as well (Imel, 1990). Electronic mail networks, such as the Adult Education Network, or AEDNET (managed by the Syracuse University Kellogg Project), facilitate the use of personal contact to identify information resources.

Searching information data bases is another common strategy for locating information. Most information data bases can be accessed both manually and by computer, and several are available in CD-ROM format. There are advantages and disadvantages to all three types of access methods. Manual searching, which refers to the process of using print indexes or catalogues to identify resources, is not as efficient as computer searching. However, it may be more effective, especially if only a small amount of material is needed or if the topic is unfamiliar. Two drawbacks to manual searching are the cost of the time devoted to the task and the fact that searching can only be done under one subject heading at a time (Imel, 1990).

If the search topic is sufficiently focused, computer searching can be both efficient and effective. It is the most efficient means of retrieving a large amount of information on a topic because it permits two or more subjects to be combined, such as literacy and evaluation or certification and adult educators. It can also allow a search to be limited in a number of ways, including by date and type of material desired, such as curricula, research materials, and so forth. Unless the topic is already focused, however, a computer search can result in irrelevant material. Because many on-line information data bases are costly to search, it may be more cost effective to have a professional searcher design and execute the search (Imel, 1990).

Searching using CD-ROM combines many of the best features of both manual and computer searching. Because there are no on-line charges being incurred, it can permit the luxury of browsing at the same time that it provides the efficiency of computer searching (Imel, 1990). Individuals who are already familiar with computers and with data-base searching will find it easy to learn to search on CD-ROM. Two disadvantages to CD-ROM searching are the tendencies to retrieve too much information and to rely too much on CD-ROM, forgetting about other reference sources (Schamber, 1988).

## Selecting Information Resources

Another skill involved in keeping abreast of information resources is the ability to select the most appropriate resources once they have been identified. Barrows (1987) suggests weighing the advantages and disadvantages of each source in terms of its availability, accessibility, and the time, effort, and money needed to acquire it. Although important in terms of the feasibility of acquiring resources, these criteria have nothing to do with evaluating the substantive nature of the resource (Imel, 1990).

Guidelines that can be used to evaluate and select resources based on their content include the following:

*Authority of the source:* Is the author an established leader in the field? Is the publisher or organization one that is known for its contributions to the field?

*Timeliness:* Is the information current and up to date? Is it based on current references?

*Relevance:* Does the source deal with the topic in a contemporary manner? Does the source contain the type of information required? Is it based on the appropriate references?

*Depth:* Is the topic treated in sufficient detail to be of use? Are the most important aspects of the topic covered?

*Accuracy:* Based on what is known about the topic, is the information correct and reliable? Is the presentation balanced?

*Replicability:* If the material will be used for the purpose of replication, does the source contain information that can be used in other settings?

When selecting the most appropriate resources, these criteria should be used as guidelines rather than as hard-and-fast rules. For example, when selecting historical materials, the criterion of timeliness would not be applied. Depending on how specific information will be used, some of these criteria will be more important than others (Imel, 1990).

## Conclusion

Changes in the way information is made available combined with the proliferation of adult education literature makes keeping up with professional resources a challenge. It may be helpful to view the process as information problem solving, which involves a series of steps (Eisenberg and Berkowitz, 1990). The first step would be to define the task—that is, to understand the problem from an "information point of view" (p. 5). In this step a logical question is "Which information sources can I bring to bear to solve the problem at hand?" The next step involves selecting the appropriate information-seeking strategies, followed by locating and accessing the information. A fourth step is selecting the most appropriate resources from among those available. A final step, to be discussed in the next two chapters, includes making effective use of the resources.

## References

Adult Learning and Literacy Clearinghouse. *Adult Education State Resource and Information Centers.* Washington, D.C.: Adult Learning and Literacy Clearinghouse, Division of Adult Education and Literacy, U.S. Department of Education, 1990.

Barrows, H. S. "Learning Management in the Context of Small Group Problem-Based Learning." In M. Cheren (ed.), *Learning Management: Emerging Directions for Learning to Learn in the Workplace.* Information Series, no. 320. Columbus, Ohio: ERIC Clearinghouse on Adult, Career, and Vocational Education, National Center for Research in Vocational Education, 1987. (ED 290 930)

Becker, H. "Can Users Really Absorb Data at Today's Rate?" *Tomorrow Data Communication,* 1986, 7, 177.

*BRS Information Technologies 1990 Database Catalog.* McLean, Va.: Maxwell Online, 1990.

Clearinghouse on Adult Education and Literacy. *Directory of National Clearinghouses: Resource Centers and Clearinghouses Serving Adult Educators and Learners.* Washington, D.C.: Clearinghouse on Adult Education and Literacy, Division of Adult Education and Literacy, U.S. Department of Education, 1990.

Cooper, H. M. *Literature Searching Strategies of Integrative Research Reviewers: A First Survey.* Columbia: University of Missouri, n.d.

*Datapro Directory of On-Line Services.* Delray, N.J.: Datapro Research Corporation, 1990.

Dialog Information Services. *DIALOG Database Catalog, 1990.* Palo Alto, Calif.: Dialog Information Services, 1990.

Eisenberg, M. B., and Berkowitz, R. E. *Information Problem Solving: The Big Skills Approach to Library and Information Skills Instruction.* Norwood, N.J.: Ablex Publishing, 1990.

*Encyclopedia of Information Systems and Services.* (10th ed.) Detroit: Gale Research Corporation, 1990.

Houle, C. *The Inquiring Mind.* Norman: Oklahoma Research Center for Continuing Professional and Higher Education, 1988. (Originally published 1961.)

Imel, S. "The Field's Literature and Information Sources." In S. B. Merriam and P. M. Cunningham (ed.), *Handbook of Adult and Continuing Education.* San Francisco: Jossey-Bass, 1989.

Imel, S. *Locating and Selecting Information: A Guide for Adult Educators.* ERIC Digest, no. 102. Columbus: ERIC Clearinghouse on Adult, Career, and Vocational Education, Center on Education and Training for Employment, Ohio State University, 1990.

*Kellogg Project Overview.* Syracuse, N.Y.: Syracuse University Kellogg Project, 1990.

Lindeman, E. *The Meaning of Adult Education.* Norman: Oklahoma Research Center for Continuing Professional and Higher Education, 1989. (Originally published 1926.)

Long, H. B. *New Perspectives on the Education of Adults in the United States.* London: Croom-Helm, 1987.

McLaughlin, P. *CD-ROM for Educators.* ERIC Digest. Syracuse, N.Y.: ERIC Clearinghouse on Information Resources, School of Education and School of Information Studies, Syracuse University, 1987.

Niemi, J. A., and Imel, S. "Information Retrieval." In C. Klevins (ed.), *Materials and Methods in Adult and Continuing Education.* Los Angeles: Klevens Publications, 1987.

Schamber, L. *The Novice User and CD-ROM Database Services.* ERIC Digest. Syracuse, N.Y.: ERIC Clearinghouse on Information Resources, School of Education and School of Information Studies, Syracuse University, 1988.

Wurman, R. *Information Anxiety.* New York: Doubleday, 1989.

*Susan Imel is director and adult education specialist at the ERIC Clearinghouse on Adult, Career, and Vocational Education, the Center on Education and Training for Employment, Ohio State University.*

*Adult and continuing educators can enhance competencies for practice and deepen understanding of the mission of adult education through knowledge of the literature.*

# Making the Most of Professional Reading

*Harold W. Stubblefield*

Practitioners in most fields of social practice are first introduced to the professional literature through formal study in professional education programs. Once they enter full-time practice, they have to develop a discipline for keeping up with the professional literature in order to maintain their competence. In adult education, however, many practitioners begin their careers without formal training. Others only gradually come to recognize that they are "doing" adult education and that they are adult educators. These practitioners need some systematic way of understanding the professional literature in order to keep up both with the literature pertaining to their specialization and with the general literature on adult education as a social practice.

How practitioners read and incorporate that reading into their working knowledge will of course vary from individual to individual. But the most effective professional reading is systematic and cumulative; occasional and unfocused reading is insufficient. To help adult educators make the most of their professional reading, this chapter identifies the domains of adult education knowledge and its literature, introduces the classics in adult education, and offers suggestions for organizing and managing a reading program. This discussion focuses specifically on books, but the suggestions presented are relevant to all kinds of reading materials. In the previous chapter, Imel presented some ideas for locating resources in adult education; this chapter explores ways to gain maximum benefit from the resources that have been located.

## Identifying the Domains of Adult Education Knowledge

The field of adult education, like other social practices, has a voluminous literature that encompasses many categories and levels of sophistication.

NEW DIRECTIONS FOR ADULT AND CONTINUING EDUCATION, no. 51, Fall 1991 ©Jossey-Bass Inc., Publishers

Because this literature treats many domains of adult education knowledge, the professional's first step in a successful reading program is to understand the nature of the literature.

**Orientation to the Literature.** Persons unfamiliar with the literature should begin their orientation with the current *Handbook of Adult and Continuing Education* (Merriam and Cunningham, 1989). This handbook provides the best one-volume introduction to adult education as a field of study and practice. It offers a cornucopia of the latest information about institutional settings, program areas, and special clientele. Recognized authorities present their ideas about facilitating learning and program operations, the contributions of various disciplines to adult education practice, and projections for the future. Readers will be introduced to the leading authorities in the field and find suggestions for more intensive study of topics that interest them.

Too big to be read at one sitting, the handbook is to be sampled at first and then studied systematically. For students in my introductory course in adult education, the handbook was an informative and challenging introduction to a new field of academic study and social practice. They began first by locating their particular institutional setting, program area, or special clientele and then moved on to explore the chapters on the foundations of practice.

Once the overviews provided by the handbook have been read, the practitioner is ready to read the more advanced scholarly and professional literature about the nature of adult education as a field of study and practice. In the context of academic disciplines, adult education is classified as a practical one; in other words, it is a discipline concerned with the use of particular means to achieve a particular end. Verner and others (1970) suggested that adult education as a practical discipline has three domains: (1) descriptive, (2) normative, and (3) procedural. An adaptation of this scheme in the subsections that follow provides an organizational framework to help practitioners understand the adult education literature. Several significant books in each of these domains are described, but this list of books is suggestive, not inclusive. The practitioner could use these suggestions to form a core library.

**Descriptive Literature.** Adult education as a descriptive discipline incorporates bodies of knowledge based on research and theory. The research methods range widely from quantitative to qualitative, from logical analysis to historical analysis. The purpose of this research is to gain an understanding of specific adult education phenomena. Although many practitioners scoff at the relevance of research, the development of effective procedures for practice depends on the quantity and quality of research and theory. A careful reading of Long's (1983) *Adult Learning: Research and Practice*—the best one-volume assessment of the adult education research literature—demonstrates the relationship between research and practice.

Researchers in adult education are concerned with several kinds of knowledge. One of the most important pertains to the nature of adults as learners; this includes such areas as adult development, motivation for learning, participation patterns, learning orientation, self-directed learning, and socioeconomic, gender, racial, or ethnic factors associated with adult learning and education. How programs are implemented, administered, and evaluated and how adult learning experiences are designed and conducted—the daily activities of practitioners—are also areas for research and theory building. History is another important area. Because present-day practices, policies, and philosophies have their origin in past events and decisions, historians serve the adult education community by providing explanations of these earlier events.

The descriptive literature tends to be technical, but it is not dry as dust nor is it unfathomable. Knox's (1977) *Adult Development and Learning* summarizes this literature and shows practitioners how to apply these findings to various situations. Belenky, Clinchy, Goldberger, and Tarule (1986) show the relevance of epistemology to adult development and to teaching in their study entitled *Women's Ways of Knowing*. Boone (1985), Houle (1972), and Mezirow, Darkenwald, and Knox (1975) illuminate program development and operational processes from the perspective of theory building, literature analysis, and empirical observation of classroom activities.

New questions about and approaches to the study of history have advanced knowledge about adult education in American society. While the older institutional histories of Grattan (1971) and Knowles (1977) are still helpful, they must be supplemented by more current research. As one example, adult education histories are now being written from the perspective of ethnicity and gender. Neufeldt and McGee's (1990) *Education of the African American Adult: An Historical Overview* provides the first comprehensive study of black adult education. No comparable work has been written about women and adult education. Blair's (1980) study of the women's club movement in the late nineteenth century from the perspective of social feminism is just one example of the illuminating studies now appearing. How adult education emerged in the 1920s and 1930s as a new educational domain in America has attracted many scholars. For example, Stubblefield's (1988) examination of the definitional history of adult education shows the wide diversity of attitudes about the meaning and social purpose of adult education in this period.

**Normative Literature.** Adult education as a practical discipline addresses the normative dimension: what should be the aims of adult education, and what are the appropriate means with which to achieve these aims? The normative literature, then, addresses such issues as the nature of adult education (definition), how do persons know (epistemology), how learners and potential learners should be treated (ethics), the purposes of adult education (social philosophy), and the allocation of resources (social policy).

For the practitioner, the challenge is to develop a philosophy to guide practice. Elias and Merriam's (1980) *Philosophical Foundations of Adult Education* is a helpful overview of several philosophies of adult education. Brookfield (1986) draws on humanistic psychology and critical theory in building his philosophy of practice in *Understanding and Facilitating Adult Learning;* his is the most constructive attempt to date to build a philosophy of adult education. In the first book-length treatment, Brockett (1988) depicts adult education practice as a process of ethical decision making. Quigley (1989) appraises the extent to which adult education as a social institution has fulfilled its promise in American society.

These are far from being esoteric concerns unrelated to the practitioner's daily task of administration, program development, or teaching. They bear directly on the populations that the practitioner's institution serves, the type of education provided, and at whose expense. Apparently routine decisions about daily operations are decisions with ethical components.

**Procedural Literature.** Adult education as a procedural discipline provides guidelines for practice, and its literature is prescriptive. This literature ranges widely from prescriptions based on uncritical descriptions of successful program practices, to prescriptions that merely reinterpret the ideas of other writers but offer little new, to prescriptions derived from systematic and critical analysis of the descriptive and normative literature.

For twenty years the most critical debate about the nature of adult education as a procedural discipline has been about the relationship of adult education to other levels and forms of education. Knowles (1980) called for adult educators to move beyond educative practices based on pedagogy (school-based practices designed for children) to andragogy— that is, educative practices based on the unique characteristics of adults as learners. The most comprehensive, one-volume introduction to the prescriptive literature based on the andragogical thesis is Knowles's *The Modern Practice of Adult Education.*

Other writers take the adult learning situation into account but also derive their prescriptions from educational psychology, learning-style research, continuing professional education, systems theory, and the analysis of adult education practice. Knox's (1986) *Helping Adults Learn* shows how a scholar draws on the current literature and on personal experience to provide specific, realistic guidance to the adult education programmer and facilitator. In *Enhancing Adult Motivation to Learn,* Wlodkowski (1985) applies motivational theory to adult learning, deriving specific principles and strategies for enhancing motivation for learning. Smith's (1982) *Learning How to Learn* addresses the problem of how to help adults become competent in managing their learning.

In the 1970s adult educators began to incorporate the newly emerging research on adult development into the literature. Adult development research provided an empirical understanding of adult life as a struggle for achievement, connections, and meaning. The descriptive depictions of the outcomes of these struggles as successful or flawed, as fulfilling or disappointing, and as healthy or unhealthy were used to create normative outcomes for age-related developmental tasks. Daloz's (1986) *Effective Teaching and Mentoring* applies developmental theory to adult learners. In this descriptively rich and personally sensitive account, Daloz shows through examples of his work with adult learners how developmental theory illuminates the holistic nature of learning for both the adult learner and the facilitator.

Beyond prescriptions for effective practice lies a more generic question about the nature of professional practice itself. What does a practitioner do when asked to provide a service to a client? How does the practitioner know what to do? Schön's (1983) *The Reflective Practitioner* creates a new paradigm of professional practice, showing how practitioners draw on knowledge derived from both research and their own experience to build a repertoire of solutions to ambiguous problems. Cervero's (1988) *Effective Continuing Education for Professionals* develops Schön's thesis and goes beyond it to explain how professionals acquire expertise and how they can maintain competence through continuing education.

## Classics in Adult Education

Several books in adult education could be called classics. By writing about their experiences in and visions of adult education, the authors of these books have produced works that are both timely and timeless. They are timely because they offer adult education or a particular form of adult education as a solution to a social maladjustment in their generation. They are timeless because their interpretation has value beyond the generation to which they spoke, and we, though removed a generation or more from the original writing, turn back to them for insight. Here are my nominations for classics in adult education since the Civil War.

**Emergence of Modern America.** New adult education forms emerged in the post–Civil War decades in response to industrialization, urbanization, immigration, and specialization. Several books produced in these decades remain as adult education classics. Written by persons with widely divergent backgrounds, the books are connected by their vision of adult education as a response to the problems of an emerging modern America. Vincent's *The Chautauqua Movement* ([1885] 1971) builds one of the earliest rationales for the systematic and organized extension of education into adulthood. He subsumes secular knowledge and culture under religious knowledge and offers a Protestant solution to economic, class, and ethnic conflicts through a program of culture. Addams's (1910) *Twenty Years at Hull House* depicts how college-educated women forged careers in social work and describes how she and others in the settlement house movement pioneered the development of progressive adult education. To the second-generation Jewish immigrants on the lower East Side of New York City, Davidson (1904) offered a cultural perspective on societal reconstruction that helped them avoid rejecting the beliefs of their parents and move beyond anarchy and socialism. *The Education of Wage Earners* contains Davidson's lectures and correspondence with his students as they tested Davidson's ideas. Arguing that intellectual ability was not a native endowment but the result of opportunity, Ward (1906), a sociologist, called for the distribution of knowledge across classes of society. His *Applied Sociology* provided the theoretical underpinnings for Van Hise's "Wisconsin Idea" of university extension.

**New Educational Domain.** In the 1920s and 1930s, adult education gained recognition as a new educational domain. Early attempts at conceptualizing this new domain focused on the problem of knowledge diffusion. Robinson (1924), a historian and a founder of the New School for Social Research, called for making the theories of natural and social scientists available to laypersons by "humanizing knowledge." Learned (1924) examined how the American public library could be an agency for diffusion of knowledge as a community intelligence center.

Attempts in this period to define the nature of adult education as an educational domain are continued in later debates about the purposes of nonvocational adult education. For example, liberal education provided the core idea for adult education, according to Martin (1926). Later, Adler (1940) introduced the American public to the "great books" as the basis for liberal education in *How to Read a Book*.

Working within the framework of progressive education, Lindeman ([1926] 1961), in *The Meaning of Adult Education,* called for an adult education that would help adults understand and respond intelligently to their life situations. In the Depression, Kotinsky (1933) defined the task of adult education from the perspective of radical progressive education. Thorndike (1928, 1935) brought experimental psychology and positivistic social science to bear on two central concerns of adult educators: adult learning ability and adult interests. Overstreet (1949) culminated three decades of study on the direction of adult development through education in *The Mature Mind*, a Book-of-the-Month Club selection and best-seller.

Bryson (1936) synthesized important ideas about adult education in the first textbook of this emerging field. Drawing on liberal education and concerned about the attempts of interest groups to propagandize for their positions, Bryson synthesized the various ideas about the purposes of adult education into the task of creating critical and independent thinkers who could submit arguments to analysis.

**Theory and Application.** It may be premature to label certain books that appeared after World War II as classics, but some of these books clearly marked turning points in adult education theory and its application to practice. Adult education theorists were deeply affected by the post–World War ll intensification of research and development; the rapid knowledge production, technological innovations, and social change that followed the war produced symptoms of "future shock" (Toffler, 1970). Preventing human obsolescence became the task of adult education after World War II. Two books prompted by this threat remain important. Knowles's (1980) *The Modern Practice of Adult Education,* first published in 1970, has already been noted. But this rationale also undergirded the work of the Commission of Professors of Adult Education in their conceptualization of adult education as a field of university study (Jensen, Liveright, and Hallenbeck, 1964).

The books published since the 1920s mark important milestones in the development of professional adult education, but in the future the search for a literature of enduring value will have to be broadened. Only recently has the role of adult education in democratic social movements been systematically studied. As adult education is increasingly perceived as part of social history, new works of enduring value may be discovered or produced about how farmers, industrial workers, women, African Americans, Native Americans, immigrants, and religious groups have created forms of adult education appropriate to their struggles.

## Reading as Professional Development

Reading is a form of professional development in which the practitioner seeks expert opinion presented in printed material. Through books, journals, research reports, and monographs, the practitioner engages in conversation with authors who are seeking to advance the knowledge of the field. Both novices and experienced practitioners recognize that organizing and following through on a reading program is not an easy task. The following suggestions from consultants, researchers, and practitioners provide specific directions for success.

**A Disposition for Reading.** Reading is a demanding intellectual activity that requires effort and open-mindedness. Readers are motivated by interest, curiosity, and need. For some, reading is a natural outgrowth of a lifelong interest in learning, and they read systematically and voraciously. Still others read sporadically, if at all. Beyond the motives of intellectual curiosity and pride in one's work, practitioners have an ethical obligation to the profession and to the learners they serve to keep up with current research, theory, and procedures. Thus, cultivating a positive attitude toward reading is essential.

**A Discipline for Reading.** A discipline for reading begins with the decision to read for professional development. Reading for professional development requires planning. Because too much literature is published each year for anyone to be able to keep up with it all, priorities have to be established. Prioritizing begins with identifying the kind of information that is needed. A time for reading professional literature has to be incorporated into the work schedule. For responsible professionals, reading is not a peripheral or optional activity. They separate professional reading from other kinds of reading, schedule time specifically for professional reading, and read at their desk. The notion of a professional development plan, discussed in Chapter Ten of this volume, can be adapted to a more specific professional reading plan.

**A Prescription for Reading.** The best way to gain access to current literature is through membership in professional associations. Practitioners in the various adult education specializations should belong to the American Association for Adult and Continuing Education, the only umbrella organization representing all segments of the field. A professional membership in this association includes subscriptions to the *Adult Education Quarterly,* the only research journal in adult education; *Adult Learning,* a popular magazine, and *Online,* a monthly newsletter.

Practitioners should also belong to the associations that focus specifically on their field of practice; these associations publish journals and newsletters. Examples of these are the American Society for Training and Development and the National University Continuing Education Association.

Bibliographies of articles and book reviews in the journals will identify additional resources. Another way of learning about books is by requesting to be placed on the mailing list of such publishers as Jossey-Bass (San Francisco), Sage (Newbury Park, California), Krieger (Malabar, Florida), and Teachers College Press (New York).

Journal and newsletter subscriptions and the buying and borrowing of books will soon produce more information than can be read. Practitioners can get control of this material by first scanning, then quickly reviewing articles and books to determine their importance. Few books should be read from cover to cover at the first reading. Read first the introduction, table of contents, and conclusion to identify the book's thesis, scope, and significance. If it seems important, then the other chapters can be read to answer further questions.

Professional reading will matter only if the information read is incorporated into one's working knowledge. Some materials will of course be copied and filed for later reference. Taking notes is a way to translate the reading experience and give it form; it also aids in understanding intellectual material (Mills, 1959).

Reading need not be strictly a private experience. Joining book clubs and journal clubs that bring together other professionals to discuss material increases one's motivation and aids in understanding and application. Brockett (1986) provides a more detailed prescription for managing professional reading.

## Conclusion

Professional reading is a form of professional development. Experienced practitioners read to keep up with the current literature and to gain new ideas for practice. Novice practitioners and more experienced practitioners who have just begun to identify themselves with the larger field of adult education should begin by understanding the structure of adult education as a field of study. For both experienced and novice practitioners, the classics of adult education show how keen minds have addressed the enduring problems of the field in ways that deserve the attention of later generations.

## References

Addams, J. *Twenty Years at Hull House.* New York: Macmillan, 1910.

Adler, M. J. *How to Read a Book: The Art of Getting a Liberal Education.* New York: Simon & Schuster, 1940.

Belenky, M. F., Clinchy, B. M., Goldberger, N. R., and Tarule, J. M. *Women's Ways of Knowing: The Development of Self, Voice, and Mind.* New York: Basic Books, 1986.

Blair, K. J. *The Clubwoman as Feminist: True Womanhood Redefined, 1868–1914.* New York: Holmes and Meier, 1980.

Boone, E. J. *Developing Programs in Adult Education.* Englewood Cliffs, N.J.: Prentice Hall, 1985.

Brockett, R. G. "Keeping Up with Professional Reading Is More than a Luxury." *Community Education Journal,* 1986, *13* (3), 9–11.

Brockett, R. G. (ed.). *Ethical Issues in Adult Education.* New York: Teachers College Press, 1988.

Brookfield, S. D. *Understanding and Facilitating Adult Learning: A Comprehensive Analysis of Principles and Effective Practices.* San Francisco: Jossey-Bass, 1986.

Bryson, L. *Adult Education.* New York: American Book Company, 1936.

Cervero, R. M. *Effective Continuing Education for Professionals.* San Francisco: Jossey-Bass, 1988.

Daloz, L. A. *Effective Teaching and Mentoring: Realizing the Transformational Power of Adult Learning Experiences.* San Francisco: Jossey-Bass, 1986.

Davidson, T. *The Education of Wage Earners.* (C. Bakewell, ed.) Boston: Ginn, 1904.

Elias, J. L., and Merriam, S. B. *Philosophical Foundations of Adult Education.* Malabar, Fla.: Krieger, 1980.

Grattan, C. H. *In Quest of Knowledge.* New York: Arno Press and the *New York Times,* 1971.

Houle, C. O. *The Design of Education.* San Francisco: Jossey-Bass, 1972.

Jensen, G., Liveright, A. A., and Hallenbeck, W. (eds.). *Adult Education: Outlines of an Emerging Field of University Study.* Washington, D.C.: Adult Education Association of the United States, 1964.

Knowles, M. S. *A History of the Adult Education Movement in the United States.* Malabar, Fla.: Krieger, 1977.

Knowles, M. S. *The Modern Practice of Adult Education.* (2nd ed.) Chicago: Follett, 1980.

Knox, A. B. *Adult Development and Learning: A Handbook on Individual Growth and Competence in the Adult Years.* San Francisco: Jossey-Bass, 1977.

Knox, A. B. *Helping Adults Learn: A Guide to Planning, Implementing, and Conducting Programs.* San Francisco: Jossey-Bass, 1986.

Kotinsky, R. *Adult Education and the Social Scene.* East Norwalk, Conn.: Appleton & Lange, 1933.

Learned, W. S. *The American Public Library and the Diffusion of Knowledge.* Orlando, Fla.: Harcourt Brace Jovanovich, 1924.

Lindeman, E. *The Meaning of Adult Education.* Montreal: Harvest House, 1961. (Originally published 1926.)

Long, H. B. *Adult Learning: Research and Practice.* New York: Cambridge, 1983.

Martin, E. D. *The Meaning of Liberal Education.* New York: Norton, 1926.

Merriam, S. B., and Cunningham, P. M. (eds.). *Handbook of Adult and Continuing Education.* San Francisco: Jossey-Bass, 1989.

Mezirow, J., Darkenwald, G. G., and Knox, A. B. *Last Gamble on Education: Dynamics of Adult Basic Education.* Washington, D.C.: Adult Education Association of the United States, 1975.

Mills, C. W. *The Sociological Imagination.* New York: Oxford University Press, 1959.

Neufeldt, H. G., and McGee, L. (eds.). *Education of the African American Adult: An Historical Overview.* Westport, Conn.: Greenwood Press, 1990.

Overstreet, H. A. *The Mature Mind.* New York: Norton, 1949.

Quigley, B. A. (ed.). *Fulfilling the Promise of Adult and Continuing Education.* New Directions for Adult and Continuing Education, no. 44. San Francisco: Jossey-Bass, 1989.

Robinson, J. H. *The Humanizing of Knowledge.* New York: Doran, 1924.

Schön, D. A. *The Reflective Practitioner.* New York: Basic Books, 1983.

Smith, R. M. *Learning How to Learn.* Chicago: Follett, 1982.

Stubblefield, H. W. *Towards a History of Adult Education in America.* London: Croom Helm, 1988.

Thorndike, E. L. *Adult Learning.* New York: Macmillan, 1928.

Thorndike, E. L. *Adult Interests.* New York: Macmillan, 1935.

Toffler, A. *Future Shock.* New York: Random House, 1970.

Verner, C., and others. *The Preparation of Adult Educators: A Selected Review of the Literature Produced in North America.* Syracuse, N.Y.: ERIC Clearinghouse on Adult Education and the Adult Education Association of the United States, 1970.

Vincent, J. H. *The Chautauqua Movement.* Freeport, N.Y.: Books for Libraries Press, 1971. (Originally published 1885.)

Ward, L. F. *Applied Sociology.* Boston: Ginn, 1906.

Wlodkowski, R. J. *Enhancing Adult Motivation to Learn: A Guide to Improving Instruction and Increasing Learner Achievement.* San Francisco: Jossey-Bass, 1985.

*Harold W. Stubblefield is professor of adult education at the Virginia Polytechnic Institute and State University.*

*How can reading research enhance professional development?*

# A Brief Guide to Critiquing Research

*Elisabeth R. Hayes*

The topic of research elicits extreme reactions from many professionals in adult and continuing education. Research is either spoken of with reverence as a source of solutions to all problems, or it is characterized as completely useless from a practical (and sometimes from a theoretical) perspective. Realistically, the value of research lies somewhere between these two extremes. The process of reading and evaluating research requires knowledge and skills that are not acquired without deliberate effort. Unfortunately, of course, research studies may be reported in a way not readily comprehensible even to other researchers. However, familiarity with some basic elements of the research process can enable practitioners to interpret and assess a good deal of the available research literature.

The purpose of this chapter is to provide readers with an overview of current research approaches in continuing education and to suggest strategies for determining the quality and utility of research findings from a practical point of view. A basic assumption is that the reader has little or no formal training in research design and methods and that she or he is primarily concerned with using research to assist in educational planning and improvement. A second assumption is that while research can be useful in such educational decision making, it cannot and should not be the only guide for practice. Sound educational decision making is contingent on a number of other factors, including explicit values and philosophical beliefs about appropriate goals of education, that cannot be verified through empirical methods. Further, all research is limited in the extent to which it can capture the complexity of human behavior and social situations. Finally, a third assumption is that this chapter alone cannot prepare readers to understand and critique all aspects of every research report. I

NEW DIRECTIONS FOR ADULT AND CONTINUING EDUCATION, no. 51, Fall 1991 © Jossey-Bass Inc., Publishers

hope, however, that it will increase awareness of the key elements of good research and encourage the reading of research as a part of professional development activities. The references at the end of the chapter provide a source of more detailed information about various research methods.

## Why Read Research?

Is taking the time both to acquire the necessary skills and to read research on a regular basis worth the effort? It is easy to argue that much adult and continuing education has proceeded relatively well with little or no apparent guidance from research. While much good practice has been and will continue to be the outcome of accumulated experience or intuitive skill, the systematic inquiry that research represents offers a potentially valuable resource as well. Contrary to popular belief, research can and does address many questions of practical significance. While research findings may not offer immediate solutions to specific practical problems, they can demonstrate the potential value of alternative strategies, challenge conventional wisdom, and offer explanations for puzzling phenomena that confront practitioners. For example, research on literacy in the workplace (Diehl and Mikulecky, 1980) indicated that job-related literacy tasks require different kinds of skills than most academic literacy tasks. This finding explained why adults with good academic literacy skills were not necessarily able to perform job-related literacy tasks. Such research had direct implications for changes in job-related adult literacy education, which previously had stressed the improvement of academic literacy skills.

Research can also suggest new ways to improve practice by indicating previously overlooked factors that may have a significant impact. For example, research on adult Hmong students (Hvitfeldt, 1986) suggests that the Hmong's culturally related styles of interaction and learning may be at odds with American educators' expectations for appropriate classroom learning. These styles may be ignored or misinterpreted if educators lack an understanding of Hmong culture; however, informed by this research, a teacher might be better able to appreciate the Hmong's preferred styles and create a supportive classroom situation for Hmong adults.

A further reason to read research lies in its ongoing impact on educational policy decisions, funding sources, development of curriculum, and other arenas that have a direct effect on practice. Often practitioners must seek out and interpret research themselves in order to respond appropriately. For example, the Adult Performance Level test and curriculum materials were based on research that may have major flaws in its conceptualization and implementation (Griffith and Cervero, 1977). Since the test and materials were commercialized and widely promoted, many practitioners had to make their own decisions about the merits of the curriculum and the study from which it was derived. Unfortunately, the widespread use of the materials suggests that the study was not subject to rigorous scrutiny by adult basic educators.

A final reason to read research lies more in the value of the process than in the content of the research itself. This chapter advocates a critical approach toward reading research. A critical approach does not consist of a negative preoccupation with identifying flaws but a thoughtful and informed consideration of both strengths and limitations in research purposes, designs, and outcomes. Unfortunately, not all published adult education research is significant, well written, or good in terms of methodology. Further, even good research is not always easy to interpret, nor are findings applicable to all settings. It takes time and thought to determine the implications for specific situations, and because of the diverse and dynamic nature of educational practice, this is not something that the researcher can do for every reader. Reading research critically, then, demands that individuals reflect on their practice as educators and on the perspectives of others. It can foster a questioning, critical attitude toward practice as well as research. Ideally such a process leads to proactive rather than reactive responses to current trends in adult and continuing education, and it supports individual professional growth.

## Understanding Different Approaches to Research

What is research? This may seem like a question with an obvious answer until one opens a research journal for the first time and encounters the diversity that exists in research design and methods. Even educational research texts offer many different definitions of research. Perhaps the best definition from a practical perspective is one that captures the essence or common ground amidst this diversity while allowing room for variation. The definition proposed by McMillan and Schumacher (1984) clarifies the key ingredients that characterize research. They state that "research is a systematic process of collecting and analyzing information (data) for some purpose" (p. 4). Two qualities of research that distinguish it from other ways of obtaining information are its purposive nature and the systematic procedures used in data collection.

Purpose and procedures are also two elements that may be used to clarify similarities and differences among research studies. In terms of purpose, research may be described as basic, applied, evaluation, or action research. *Basic research* is "research done to test theory, to study relationships among phenomena in order to understand the phenomena, with little or no thought of applications of the results of the research to practical problems" (Kerlinger, 1979, p. 283). In contrast, *applied research* is conducted in a field of common practice and is concerned with the development and application of research-based knowledge about those practices. Applied research is intended to address a general problem in a particular field; its purpose is not to suggest specific strategies for practice (McMillan and Schumacher, 1984). The purpose of *evaluation research* is to assess the merits of existing practices in a clearly defined setting. *Action research,* while sometimes characterized as a research method, also represents yet another purpose: to develop and test solutions to specific problems encountered in practice.

While research that addresses immediate practical issues might seem to be most relevant for practitioners, even basic research can have great utility. For example, research on adult cognition (Rybash, Hoyer, and Roodin, 1986), while not focused on educational questions, nonetheless has important implications for the design of learning strategies in many continuing education settings.

Another way of understanding differences in research is to consider the procedures used to collect and analyze information. Typically, a contrast is made between *quantitative* and *qualitative* methods. These procedures are associated with different philosophical assumptions about the nature of knowledge and how research might contribute to knowledge. Quantitative research is based on principles of the positivist philosophy of science. These principles include the assumption that valid knowledge is acquired only through objective observation of external phenomena. A primary task of the researcher is to gather empirical data as a means of testing general theories, such as those about human behavior. Key concerns are identification and isolation of relevant variables and precise measurement of phenomena. A typical goal is to establish the generalizability of research findings across situations or for groups of individuals.

In contrast, qualitative research is based on a naturalistic or postpositivistic philosophy in which it is assumed that knowledge is "the creation of the human mind. It is not out there to be discovered" (Deshler and Hagan, 1989, p. 149). From this perspective, data about external phenomena are insufficient for an adequate understanding of human behavior. Information about the subjective perspectives of those involved in the research is considered essential to a real understanding of individuals and social situations. Not only does the researcher strive to understand the perspectives of the research subjects but she or he also acknowledges how her or his own preconceptions and assumptions affect interpretations of the data. Rather than using a priori theory as a guide for research, a goal is the creation of "grounded theory"—theory that is developed from the data. An emphasis is placed on collecting information in a holistic manner about human beings in natural settings rather than on isolating and measuring variables in controlled settings or with standardized measures. Typically there is more concern with developing comprehensive descriptions of the research subjects and setting rather than with making generalizations to other people or situations.

The degree to which these two perspectives represent discrete and incompatible alternatives remains a topic of debate. It is possible, for example, to find research that utilizes both quantitative and qualitative methods of data collection. While the distinction between quantitative and qualitative may not be a completely adequate means of categorizing research, awareness of these different underlying assumptions and corresponding methods is important since they suggest different criteria to use in evaluating research design and outcomes. For example, while evidence of predetermined, standard procedures for data collection can be critical in establishing the quality of a quantitative study, a good qualitative study might show evidence of interview or observation strategies that emerged gradually as the researcher gained new insight into the research topic.

## Research Methods

In this section, a number of commonly used research methods associated with quantitative and qualitative approaches are described briefly. In each description, a few key points to consider when evaluating such research are noted.

**Survey Methods.** One of the most commonly used quantitative research methods in adult and continuing education is the survey design. Surveys provide descriptive information about individual and group characteristics, attitudes, behavior, or other variables or about potential relationships between variables, such as between age and participation in education. A common error in the interpretation of survey data is confusion between correlations and the existence of causes and effects; usually it is difficult to establish causal relationships with this method. Typical goals of surveys are generalizations about a larger group or population based on data from a subgroup or sample of that population. Accordingly, survey research reports should include not only a description of how the sample was selected but also evidence that the sample is comparable to the population to which the findings are to be generalized.

Another concern in survey research is the quality of the data collection procedures. Data are typically collected through the use of questionnaires or interviews. Evidence of the reliability and validity of these instruments and procedures should be provided. *Reliability* is "the consistency of a measurement, the extent to which the results are similar over different forms of the same instrument or occasions of data collecting" (McMillan and Schumacher, 1984, p. 126). To establish reliability, researchers relate the results from one set of measurements to those from a second set; the greater the correlation, the greater the reliability. A number of different statistical procedures may be used to estimate reliability. One commonly used procedure is to look for *internal consistency* by correlating responses on half the items on an instrument with responses from the other half.

*Validity* is more difficult to establish. The essence of validity is the answer to the question, "Are you measuring what you think you are measuring?" (Kerlinger, 1979, p. 138). A number of different kinds of validity are important in educational research. *Content validity* refers to whether the items or questions on a measure adequately represent the variable or phenomena under investigation. Kerlinger (1979) provides a cogent discussion of other types of validity.

As these points suggest, survey research may seem relatively straightforward, but determining the quality of a survey research study is not that simple. Often-cited examples of large-scale survey research include Johnstone and Rivera's (1965) and Aslanian and Brickell's (1980) studies of participation in continuing education; Boshier's (1971) research on motivations; and Darkenwald and Valentine's (1985) research on deterrents to participation.

**Experimental and Quasi-Experimental Methods.** Unlike most survey research, experimental research has the primary goal of establishing cause-and-effect relationships, such as between the use of learning contracts and enhanced learning outcomes. *Independent variables* are manipulated by the researcher to determine their effect on *dependent variables*. The variables and relationships to be investigated are typically described in a statement of one or more hypotheses. In a true experimental study, the researcher randomly assigns subjects to experimental or control groups. The experimental groups receive a particular "treatment"—for example, contract learning. The control group does not experience the treatment but in all other respects is subject to comparable conditions. Impact of the treatment on one or more dependent variables—in this case, learning outcomes—is then assessed by making comparisons between the treatment and control groups. Important in this kind of research is the identification and control of extraneous factors that might also lead to differences between the groups.

Clearly, this kind of design is difficult to use in most real-world situations. For example, researchers may need to conduct studies using classes of students that are not randomly assigned. In such studies, called quasi-experimental research, researchers employ strategies that compensate for the inability to assign subjects randomly to groups. However, the potential effects of uncontrolled differences between groups become even more problematic. Both true experimental studies and quasi-experimental studies are relatively rare in adult education research. One example in a continuing professional education setting is the work of Rosenblum and Darkenwald (1983). While the difficulty in obtaining controlled situations and the complexity of human behavior can make it difficult to establish the accuracy of conclusions based on experimental research, such studies can be valuable in cases where a controlled setting was possible.

**Ethnographic Methods.** Ethnography as a research strategy has its origins in anthropology, and in its "pure" form it retains an emphasis on describing the culture of a particular situation. Ethnographic research is characterized by the use, often in combination, of various qualitative methods, such as observations, interviews, and analysis of written and nonwritten materials, in order to collect extensive information about people in natural settings. Frequently the subjects of the research are purposively selected on the basis of unique or distinctive qualities, rather than as representatives of a larger population. Unlike survey or experimental research, data collection procedures are open-ended, and the design of the study can develop and change as the research progresses. The researcher is considered to be the primary data collection tool in that he or she relies heavily on his or her powers of observation and interpretation in compiling and analyzing data. A rigorous process of comparative analysis is used to identify patterns of meaning in the data.

According to Wolcott (1988, p. 89), "the ultimate test of an ethnography lies in the adequacy of its explanation rather than the power of its method." A key quality to look for in an ethnographic study, then, is the meaningfulness of the concepts or theory that are derived from the data. Also important are the richness and vividness of the description; detailed examples and direct quotations are commonly used to support the researcher's interpretations. The study by Hvitfeldt (1986) cited earlier is one example of ethnographic research in adult education; others include Mezirow, Darkenwald, and Knox (1975) and Fingeret (1983).

**Case Study Methods.** Case study research can be characterized by a focus on a "bounded system" (Stake, 1988, p. 255): an individual, group, institution, or other social entity that has a clearly defined identity. The overall purpose of such research is to develop a comprehensive understanding of that entity. Merriam (1988) identifies three kinds of case studies according to their ultimate end product: descriptive, interpretive, and evaluative. Descriptive case studies offer basic information about phenomena, without the purpose of verifying or developing theory. In contrast, interpretive case studies go beyond description by generating new concepts or testing the adequacy of existing theory. Evaluative case studies attempt to judge the "worth" of phenomena as well as to describe and explain them. To achieve these ends, qualitative methods are most commonly used, although quantitative data can also be appropriate.

One recent example of a case study in adult education is provided by Johnston (1985), who describes the impact of psychological and social factors on the reading difficulties experienced by three adult men with limited literacy skills. A second example is Belsheim's (1986) analysis of the organizing patterns of three continuing professional education centers. It is always important to be cautious in assuming or accepting claims that case study findings can be applied to other cases; this kind of research is not designed to be generalized to other populations. As with other qualitative methods, case study research is perhaps most appropriate for suggesting new concepts and explanations rather than for making generalizations.

**Historical Methods.** Historical research is growing in popularity in the adult education literature. While historical studies might seem to have less practical utility than other kinds of research, there are a number of unique contributions that such research can make to practice. For example, knowledge of history can enable us to understand better the relationship between continuing education practice and its changing sociocultural context.

Unlike the methods already described, it is more difficult to characterize historical methods. In fact, as Kaestle (1988) observes, there is not one readily definable approach to historical inquiry. Instead, what appears to unite historical research is its goal of understanding the past through the investigation of historical materials.

Key concerns in evaluating historical research pertain to the quality of the source material and the researcher's interpretation of information. The genuineness of the source material itself must be established, and potential errors or bias in sources should be noted. When assessing the historian's interpretation of the material, readers should be particularly sensitive to inaccuracies due to *presentism:* "the tendency to interpret past events using concepts and perspectives that originated in more recent times" (Borg and Gall, 1989, p. 825).

Rose's (1989) study is a useful example of historical research in adult education. Drawing on archival material, including conference proceedings, letters, and reports, she analyzes the Carnegie Corporation's role in the founding of the American Association for Adult Education. Rachal (1988) and Rohfeld (1990) provide additional examples of historical research; Hugo (1990) offers a valuable discussion of gender bias in historical research on adult education.

**Participatory Research.** Participatory research differs from other research methods in a number of ways. Central to this approach is the active participation of people in the acquisition of knowledge that they can use for self-empowerment. Participatory research typically has the ultimate goal of enabling participants to challenge and transform inequitable social and political structures. The process consists of collective investigation and analysis of immediate problems and of collective action to implement solutions. While participatory research commonly takes place in nonformal adult education settings in developing nations, such research can be found in industrialized settings as well. For example, *Participatory Research* (Society for Participatory Research in Asia, 1982) describes how a coalition of citizen's groups in Appalachia organized and conducted a six-state study of land ownership. As one outcome, the citizens were able to use the information to fight land abuse by absentee corporations.

It is difficult to evaluate participatory research studies. The results of such research are not intended for generalization to other settings; what is perhaps of most value to readers is the example of how the research process contributed to positive change for the individuals involved.

## What Makes Good Research?

While these descriptions include some essential elements of good research specific to each method, there are also some common criteria that can be used to evaluate research studies in general. These criteria pertain to research reporting and the substance of the research.

**Research Reporting.** Initial criteria for a good research report lie in how adequately the research process is described. If the process is not well documented, its quality in relation to other criteria cannot be assessed. The process of most research can be divided into identifying a problem, establishing a conceptual framework, specifying the phenomena to be studied, selecting and using a particular method of data collection, and analyzing data (Merriam and Simpson, 1984). Each of these elements should be described in the research report. For example, a typical quantitative research report should include an introduction, problem statement, literature review, specific research questions or hypotheses, description of sample selection procedures and characteristics, description of data collection and analysis procedures, findings and interpretation or discussion of findings, and implications. A qualitative research study might be reported in a somewhat less linear fashion, without formal hypotheses or objectives, but all aspects of the research process should still be described.

**Substance of the Research Study.** Only if the research is adequately reported is it possible to assess the substance of the study. One key criterion in evaluating substance is the significance of the research problem or of the questions that were addressed by the study. There are no clear-cut guidelines for assessing the significance of a particular study, and it is certain that what is significant to one person may seem unimportant or irrelevant to another. However, part of the task of the research report is to demonstrate the significance of the study to readers. This should be done both directly by stating its significance or importance and indirectly by providing evidence of how the study meets a need for new information. A literature review or conceptual framework that is clearly relevant to the problem should clarify the rationale for the study. Generally, significance can be assessed by the extent to which the research contributes to the improvement of practice and theory in continuing education. If the problem is not significant, even a well-crafted study has little value.

The next aspect to consider is the actual execution of the research. An initial question to ask is whether the overall methodology appears to be appropriate for an investigation of the identified problem. Three aspects of the study can then be assessed: selection of subjects; data collection; and analysis. The sample should be selected in a manner appropriate to the problem and overall methodology; the size of the sample should also correspond to the goals of the research. Consider whether the characteristics of the sample suggest that it is biased in any way. If so, be sure to note how such bias might affect the findings of the study and its overall worth. Any data collection instruments should be fully described and appropriate for the sample. Inaccurate findings can result from the use of questionnaires or tests developed for populations significantly different from the research sample. Evidence of reliability and validity, discussed earlier, should be provided for tests and questionnaires. Were data analysis techniques utilized appropriately? While a reader may not be able to evaluate the more technical aspects of such techniques, she or he can determine if procedures were used that addressed the purpose of the research and if any obvious variables were overlooked.

A number of questions should be asked to evaluate the interpretation of findings. Do all interpretations and implications have a clear basis in the data or previous research and theory? Does the researcher avoid unreasonable claims about generalizability of the findings? Are the limitations of the study acknowledged? Are alternative explanations of findings discussed?

Finally, readers need to ask themselves some questions about the relevance of the study to their own professional practice. For example, if a teacher's goal is to apply research findings about classroom learning to a particular setting, she must consider how different the research sample is from her own students and whether those differences are likely to affect the applicability of the research. The results of some research might not suggest specific strategies but might be useful in a more global sense if its relevance to the development and design of programs and learning activities is considered.

## How to Read a Research Report

There is no one best way to read a research report; the best strategy is to develop a personal style. However, there are some general approaches to avoid as well as a few strategies that can lead to more effective reading.

*Wrong Way Number One.* (1) Skip the abstract since you are going to read the article. (2) Begin reading carefully at the introduction, trying to understand every word. (3) Look back at the references whenever there is a citation in the text. (4) Make sure that you understand every statistic and every table, if any, as you read. Spend considerable time on this. (5) Stop when you don't understand all the terminology or statistics. Don't continue until you find a reference book or an expert to help you.

*Wrong Way Number Two.* (1) Read the title of the report or article. (2) Only if the title is interesting, read the abstract. (3) If the abstract is really intriguing, read the section on implications. After all, you are only interested in applying research findings, not in doing research.

These represent extreme but perhaps not unusual approaches to reading research. The second may be more common than the first approach simply because most people (including expert researchers) would, at best, find the first way tedious and at worst would never finish any article for fear of not understanding each detail. However, the second approach can be quite ineffective because the reader might (1) miss articles of real interest and relevance (titles often cannot convey the real substance of the study), (2) try to use results of research that is flawed or not generalizable to his or her setting, (3) miss implications that the researcher did not provide, and (4) miss the chance to learn about other relevant research and alternative perspectives that might be mentioned elsewhere in the study.

**A Better Way to Read Research.** Here is one general approach to use: (1) Skim the abstract to get an overview of the study and an initial sense of the research design. (2) Then read the introduction, problem statement, and conclusion. This will provide an indication of the significance of the study and its findings. (3) If the study still seems to be of interest, then read it more thoroughly for meaning. Look for general signs that the study is well done. If you plan to utilize the findings in some way, you should read it carefully again to assess its credibility in a more thorough manner. At this point, you should be sure that you understand most terminology and details of the study.

**How to Read Statistics (for Nonstatisticians).** Statistical data and terminology can be particularly disconcerting for a novice reader of research. Anyone who is seriously trying to read and understand research will need to consult additional references to become familiar with commonly used statistical procedures; however, a few broad guidelines may be helpful when evaluating statistically based research. In general, errors can exist in the selection and use of statistical procedures and in the interpretation of statistical test results. First, it is necessary to clarify the purpose of the statistical procedures and determine whether they are appropriate given the research questions or hypotheses. A basic statistical or research methods text can be used to check the purpose of unfamiliar methods. Kerlinger (1979) offers a readable explanation of basic statistical methods using a conceptual approach. It is also important to determine if the sample size is adequate for the statistical methods used. Keep in mind that with small samples, a few atypical subjects or extreme responses can have a big impact on the overall statistics for the group. Research texts usually suggest minimum numbers for the appropriate use of specific procedures.

If the procedures are appropriate, then the researcher's interpretation of the findings can be assessed. A frequent problem is lack of distinction between statistical significance and practical significance. *Statistical significance* indicates the likelihood that a particular association or difference between measurements would occur by chance. *Practical significance* has to do with whether such associations or differences are meaningful in terms of their potential impact on educational practice. For example, research might show that there is a statistically significant difference in response time of older adults and younger adults on a test of cognitive skill; if the difference is only a few seconds, the practical significance of such findings is obviously minimal. This is particularly an issue when large samples are used, since small differences in these cases can yield statistically significant results. Thus, it is important to consider both the level of statistical significance as well as the actual scores or responses on which the findings were based.

## Conclusion

The serious reader will need more information than could be covered in this chapter in order to critique research studies adequately. Helpful general texts on research methods include Merriam and Simpson (1984) and Borg and Gall (1989). Jaeger's (1988) text includes explanations of seven research procedures as well as sample research studies in education. These overviews provide detailed references to texts on specific methods.

## References

Aslanian, C. B., and Brickell, H. M. *Americans in Transition: Life Changes as Reasons for Adult Learning.* New York: College Entrance Examination Board, 1980.

Belsheim, D. J. "Organizing Continuing Professional Education: A Comparative Case Analysis." *Adult Education Quarterly,* 1986, 36, 211-225.

Borg, W. R., and Gall, M. D. *Educational Research: An Introduction.* White Plains, N.Y.: Longman, 1989.

Boshier, R. "Motivational Orientations of Adult Education Participants: A Factor Analytic Exploration of Houle's Typology." *Adult Education,* 1971, 21, 3-26.

Darkenwald, G. G., and Valentine, T. "Factor Structure of Deterrents to Participation in Adult Education." *Adult Education Quarterly,* 1985, 35, 177-193.

Deshler, D., with Hagan, N. "Adult Education Research: Issues and Directions." In S. B. Merriam and P. M. Cunningham (eds.), *Handbook of Adult and Continuing Education.* San Francisco: Jossey-Bass, 1989.

Diehl, W. A., and Mikulecky, L. "The Nature of Reading at Work." *Journal of Reading,* 1980, 24, 221-227.

Fingeret, A. "Social Network: A New Perspective on Independence and Illiterate Adults." *Adult Education Quarterly,* 1983, 33, 133-146.

Griffith, W. S., and Cervero, R. M. "The Adult Performance Level Program: A Serious and Deliberate Examination." *Adult Education,* 1977, 27, 209-224.

Hugo, J. M. "Adult Education History and the Issue of Gender: Toward a Different History of Adult Education in America." *Adult Education Quarterly,* 1990, 41, 1-16.

Hvitfeldt, C. "Traditional Culture, Perceptual Style, and Learning: The Classroom Behavior of Hmong Adults." *Adult Education Quarterly,* 1986, 36, 65-77.

Jaeger, R. M. (ed.). *Complementary Methods for Research in Education.* Washington, D.C.: American Educational Research Association, 1988.

Johnston, P. H. "Understanding Reading Disability: A Case Study Approach." *Harvard Educational Review,* 1985, 55, 153-177.

Johnstone, J.W.C., and Rivera, R. J. *Volunteers for Learning: A Study of Educational Pursuits of American Adults.* Hawthorne, N.Y.: Aldine, 1965.

Kaestle, C. "Recent Methodological Developments in the History of American Education." In R. M. Jaeger (ed.), *Complementary Methods for Research in Education.* Washington, D.C.: American Educational Research Association, 1988.

Kerlinger, F. N. *Behavioral Research: A Conceptual Approach.* Troy, Mo.: Holt, Rinehart & Winston, 1979.

McMillan, J. H., and Schumacher, S. *Research in Education: A Conceptual Introduction.* Boston: Little, Brown, 1984.

Merriam, S. B. *Case Study Research in Education: A Qualitative Approach.* San Francisco: Jossey-Bass, 1988.

Merriam, S. B., and Simpson, E. *A Guide to Research for Educators and Trainers of Adults.* Malabar, Fla.: Krieger, 1984.

Mezirow, J., Darkenwald, G. G., and Knox, A. *Last Gamble on Education.* Washington, D.C.: Adult Education Association of the United States, 1975.

Rachal, J. R. "Gutenberg, Literacy, and the Ancient Art of Memory." *Adult Education Quarterly,* 1988, *38,* 125–135.

Rohfeld, R. W. "James Harvey Robinson: Historian as Adult Educator." *Adult Education Quarterly,* 1990, *40,* 219–228.

Rose, A. D. "Beyond Classroom Walls: The Carnegie Corporation and the Founding of the American Association for Adult Education." *Adult Education Quarterly,* 1989, *39,* 140–151.

Rosenblum, S., and Darkenwald, G. G. "Effects of Adult Learner Participation in Course Planning on Achievement and Satisfaction." *Adult Education Quarterly,* 1983, *33,* 147–153.

Rybash, J. M., Hoyer, W. J., and Roodin, P. A. *Adult Cognition and Aging.* Elmsford, N.Y.: Pergamon Press, 1986.

Society for Participatory Research in Asia. *Participatory Research: An Introduction.* Khanpur, New Delhi, India: Society for Participatory Research in Asia, 1982.

Stake, R. E. "Case Study Methods in Educational Research: Seeking Sweet Water." In R. M. Jaeger (ed.), *Complementary Methods for Research in Education.* Washington, D.C.: American Educational Research Association, 1988.

Wolcott, H. "Ethnographic Research in Education." In R. M. Jaeger (ed.), *Complementary Methods for Research in Education.* Washington, D.C.: American Educational Research Association, 1988.

*Elisabeth R. Hayes is assistant professor of adult education at the University of Wisconsin, Madison.*

*Sharing ideas in print is a professional responsibility of educators of adults in the information age; a number of strategies can help new writers get their work published.*

# Getting Ideas into Print: Some Tips for Practitioners

*Rodney D. Fulton*

Publishing is an activity that has always had an aura of mystery about it. Relatively few individuals actually have their work published. To be honest, publishing is a very competitive activity. Leaving publications to the "experts," practitioners too often do not accept the challenge of writing. Those involved in the day-to-day activities of adult education possess a wealth of information and perspectives that need to be communicated with large audiences. Conference presentations are one way to accomplish this; however, publishing is another critical activity. In this information age, the production of ideas has become crucial to society, and sharing both the process and the product of idea development has become a responsibility for the professional. This chapter offers practitioners a new model for writing and maintains that publication is vital to professional development.

## Why Should I Write?

In many fields, practitioners criticize the literature as being controlled by academicians who engage primarily in research rather than in the practice of their discipline. This criticism is often valid. However, practitioners cannot simply ignore their responsibility to contribute just because publication has been inaccessible to them. Practitioners need to take a more assertive role in professional publication—by developing their writing and by submitting manuscripts—in order for the professional literature to begin to reflect both research and practice. Contributions from both academicians and practitioners can strengthen the quality of professional adult education literature.

But practitioners need to write not just to improve the quality of professional literature. Practitioners can bring an important quality to publications by reflecting the experiences of adult learners and educators. The purpose of writing, for both academicians and practitioners, should be to express ideas, concerns, comments, and information that are beneficial to the learning community. One must be able to write well in order to be published; however, the purpose of publication should not be simply to impress colleagues with that ability but rather to share ideas with others so that the adult education enterprise can be advanced.

Certainly, the satisfaction of a job well done is another reason for publishing. The sense of achievement that comes from successful negotiation of the publishing process and from seeing one's work in print needs to be acknowledged as an important reason to undergo the arduous task of writing for professional publication. The thrill of seeing one's ideas (and name) in print makes the task worthwhile.

## Who Should Write?

Any educator of adults who is willing to devote the time and effort to the task of writing and the process of publishing should write. One should not attempt to write professionally if the time is not available for this activity. On the other hand, Henson (1987, p. 10) said, "The response of successful writers is, 'I don't find time for it. I just do it.' " This attitude is echoed by several others (Atchity, 1986; Becker, 1986; Van Til, 1986): good writers make writing such a priority that time for writing happens—not without sacrifice, but it does happen. O'Neill (1990) suggested that viewing professional writing just as one would a report written for the boss with a firm deadline will help in being published.

In a research design class I co-taught during the summer of 1988, one of the final discussions dealt with publishing research. I looked out at the participants and saw mostly incredulous looks. One student even admitted what she was thinking: maybe someone else in this class would publish, but she never would. The following fall, that individual received a Phi Delta Kappa research grant and conducted a study on the effect of using simulations in classroom enrichment activity. As I performed the statistical analysis with her, I again suggested that she publish this local study. I managed to convince her that her final report to Phi Delta Kappa, with some revisions, could be submitted for publication. The article was recently published in a national social studies periodical.

When first offered the opportunity to publish in the proceedings of a conference several years ago, I turned it down, saying that I would never have time as a busy education specialist in the Army Continuing Education System to write anything worth publishing. To this day, I regret that I did not take the time to put into writing what I had presented to a small group in New York. The answer to the question posed in the heading, then, is that anyone should write who recognizes that the time and effort required are part of his or her professional responsibility to help advance the field of adult and continuing education.

## Two Common Myths About Writing

There are many commonly held beliefs about writing and publication. Some of these are based on reality, but others may be myths that have developed over the years. Two of these myths, actually opposite sides of the same coin, need to be challenged by educators of adults as they publish professionally.

**Myth Number One: Everyone Can Write.** In a democratic society, some tend to believe that everyone can do everything. In fact, in a democracy, all should be afforded equal opportunity, but this does not guarantee equal results. The simple reality is that not everyone can write well enough to publish. There are three prerequisite skills for a published writer: a command of the written language, a message to communicate, and the discipline and desire to write that message.

Individuals lacking any of these skills need not give up on being published, however. Gay and Edgil (1990, p. 461) contend that "having one's work evaluated as poorly written can be a blow to the ego, but it is probably the easiest reason for rejection that can be overcome." There are many strategies for improving one's writing skills. Practitioners of adult education should be aware of both formal and informal opportunities, including college classes, writing support groups, and seminars or workshops. *Improving Your Writing Skills* (Apps, 1982) is another excellent resource.

Another strategy is to write one's ideas down and then submit the manuscript to others for review. This strategy is helpful for all writers, not just those who need to develop their writing skills. O'Neill (1990) suggests that in addition to using good writing techniques, such as outlining and revising, one's chances of successful publication are increased when the manuscript is reviewed by several people before submission. In dealing with a rejected manuscript, Gay and Edgil (1990, p. 459) suggest, "It is important that you do not let embarrassment prohibit you from sharing the manuscript and editorial critique with one or more colleagues for their opinions." The author will have to decide when collegial review prior to submission warrants co-authorship, but the value of peer review cannot be overstated.

**Myth Number Two: Only Academicians Can Publish.** The inverse of the myth that everyone can write for publication is that only those with advanced degrees possess the skills to publish. Perhaps some individuals facing promotion and tenure boards with requirements for publication view it as the sacred turf of the scholarly. However, today's publishing world does not validate this myth. Those without a Ph.D. or Ed.D. may find it tougher to gain access to professional publication. Yet the lack of such a degree cannot be used as an excuse to avoid attempting to publish. This book and others in the New Directions series have chapters written by individuals without their doctorate. Graduate students and practitioners do write and publish in a wide range of sources. For example, every year a few dissertations result in other scholarly articles, and many professors of adult education encourage students to produce manuscripts based on their dissertation study.

Many individuals are becoming more involved in the professional literature in other ways. Currently, graduate students at Syracuse University, along with students from several other institutions, are publishing an electronic journal, *New Horizons in Adult Education.* The editor and review board, all graduate students, accept submissions from both graduate students and nonstudents. During my first three years of graduate study, I published several book reviews, three commissioned reports for Kellogg Centers, three articles, had four manuscripts accepted for *Resources in Education,* and was invited to contribute chapters to two books. While graduate students must balance the commitment to write for publication with the commitment to complete a program of studies, it is possible to do both.

Practitioners of adult education also have opportunities to publish. Journals that describe themselves as primarily for educators rather than researchers include articles from practitioners whose writing is usually not constrained by the pressure to publish or perish. Newsletters and reports are other possible outlets for sharing ideas. While these publications are not refereed or considered "professional," they are nonetheless important sources of information for practitioners.

Among the publications that are oriented toward practice rather than research are *Adult Learning,* which actively seeks contributions from practitioners rather than academicians, the *Journal of Extension,* and the *Community Education Journal.* Practitioners publish in order to share ideas rather than for promotion and tenure, and they thus have available to them a whole world of publishing opportunities that may not be attractive to academicians.

## Writing Should Be "FUN"

What does a practitioner of adult and continuing education do after determining that he or she has the time and the skill to write? A successful writer needs to engage in three simultaneous activities: *focusing, understanding,* and *networking.* One might say that successful writers have "FUN"!

**Writing Is Focusing.** The successful writer, whether an academician or a practitioner, needs to focus on the "what, when, and where" of writing activity. The literature is full of references to how important it is to establish a place for writing. While some give specific suggestions for where that place should be, I suggest that writing is such a personal endeavor that where one writes must reflect the individual. Whether it is an office location, a study at home, a public library, or an outdoor retreat is not crucial. But it is important to have a place that one knows is for writing. Atchity (1986) proclaimed that "you must have complete control over the surroundings in which you write daily" (p. 136). He continued, "People are often unaware of the unconscious choices they make about work space. Conscious knowledge of your preferences allows you to control your productivity" (p. 139).

Another focus of the writer must be time. When one writes is as varied as is the human personality; we all know people who do everything best first thing in the morning and others who cannot function until late at night. Van Til (1986, p. 154) pointed out that "amateur writers constantly inquire about writers' ways of working. Surely there must be some magic time or place or even quill! They never learn that there are no 'secrets.' " While there may be no secrets, there is simple common sense—write when and where one is able to be the most productive.

Focusing on the time and place of writing is simply paying attention to the physical nature of this task. Successful writers realize the flaw in "conventional thinking about writing [that] distinguishes the thinking part, which brings prestige to the person who does it, from the physical part, which doesn't" (Becker, 1986, p. 152). These writers recognize that "being a mental activity doesn't mean that writing is only mental. Like every other activity, it has a physical side, and that side affects the thinking part more than we usually admit" (Becker, 1986, p. 152).

One of the most intimidating aspects of writing is focusing on what to write. Once again, there are no secrets, simply common sense. One should develop ideas for publication out of one's own experience. O'Neill (1990, p. 37) says it concisely: "Write about what you know." Graduate students early on in their studies can find a topic that interests them, can use that topic for papers in various classes—in effect, writing variations on the same theme—and then can turn some part of this concentrated effort into a dissertation proposal. Along the way, this research can also result in book reviews, and well-written papers can turn into journal submissions. This is not to say that every paper for a graduate course is publishable. Both student and professor need to invest extra effort and time in order to reach the goal of publishing a student's paper. But it can be done. Three of the book reviews I published as a graduate student began as course assignments, and two of my course papers were accepted for publication.

In deciding what to write, practitioners should reflect on methods, techniques, and ideas that are grounded in their daily work. Sharing the successes and problems that occur in adult education can result in useful information for other educators of adults. The student mentioned earlier, who thought she would never publish, actually wrote about her work in gifted and talented education in the local school system, not about some theoretical idea.

**Writing Is Understanding.** There are four basic understandings that can lead to greater success in writing. First, writers must understand their writing styles. How one writes—the choice of words, the combination of words into sentences, the organization of sentences into paragraphs both grammatically and logically—impacts the message that one conveys. A writer should not attempt to copy some other style but rather to understand and be comfortable with his or her own. The only requirement is that the message be clear, concise, and well developed. How well developed? Well enough to say what needs to be said within the space limitations of the publication.

Second, it is crucial that a writer understand the audience and write for that particular group, not for all educators or adult learners. Writers should select a specific target for publication, read several past copies, and know to whom this publication is sent. If writing in a journal for instructors of English as a Second Language (ESL), for example, one should write specifically to them. Not only does this process help to target the message clearly but it also leaves room for rewriting the piece for different groups of readers.

Third, if one is ever to see a manuscript published, one needs to understand the potential sources of publication. At a minimum, one must be knowledgeable of and follow to the letter all publication and style requirements. In addition, a writer needs to know the focus of the journal to which a manuscript is sent. Sending a "how-to" piece to a research journal is not a productive activity for either author or editor.

The fourth important understanding for an author is knowing what one can contribute to the question being considered in the manuscript. There are at least five ways to contribute to the literature. First, one may want to review the current state of knowledge on a particular subject. In this case, reviewing the work of others in an organized fashion is appropriate. Second, an author may wish to synthesize what others have written into a unified statement. Third, an author may be suggesting some new relationship among established ideas. Fourth, the author may be suggesting a completely new concept or technique. Fifth, the author may wish to report original research findings. Clearly understanding at which level one is attempting to write allows for a concise yet thorough development of the manuscript.

**Writing Is Networking.** Many Americans have been taught that cooperative learning is not the preferred method and that individual work, especially in writing, is the right choice. In the information age, this mindset needs to be challenged. This is not, of course, to suggest any changes in the ethics of writing nor to condone plagiarism. Becker (1986, p. 19) wrote, "Because most people write in absolute privacy, readers attribute the results to the author alone." What is needed is a conscious awareness that writing is a group effort in many ways, even if not in the putting of ideas onto paper or into the computer file.

One way successful authors network is by reading. Active reading allows an author to be aware of what others are saying in the field. Staying abreast of the field can be viewed as a professional responsibility, but it also avoids the potential embarrassment of trying to say the same old thing one more time. Reading is a crucial part of the experience authors need in order to analyze the ideas of others critically and to integrate their own ideas with those of other professional educators of adults. Chapters Two and Three in this volume address this aspect of networking in greater detail.

Another way successful authors network is face to face. Meeting other professionals so that a name can be associated with a face in no way hurts one's chances for publication. The support and exposure that attending conferences and workshops can generate can be a boost to one's attempts to be published. Being active in professional groups, such as the American Association for Adult and Continuing Education, the American Society for Training and Development, and Phi Delta Kappa, is vital to a professional career for many reasons, and certainly one of them is that it may help in getting published. Chapter Seven discusses this aspect of professional networking. This is not to support the adage that who one knows is more important than what one knows; it simply affirms that a reputation can help. In addition, an excellent publication can result from writing based on a presentation. Successfully presenting at a conference or meeting gives one immediate feedback from the participants. This feedback can be helpful in producing a written manuscript for submission. Of course, one must always find out if proceedings are going to be published based on an abstract submitted prior to the presentation or if one will be given the opportunity to submit an article afterward.

We are fortunate that technology affords another way to network. Using electronic mail and computer-assisted discussion groups such as those developed by the Kellogg Project at Syracuse University allows one to exchange ideas with a much wider group than is possible through face-to-face contact. Often, the computer is praised as the salvation of harried authors because of word processing; however, modems may be a much more dramatic aid to the author because they put people in touch so easily. Today, business cards for educators of adults frequently carry electronic mail addresses as well as the traditional work address or telephone number.

Computers serve the potential author in two other ways. First, while experiencing the pains of a relatively new form, electronic publishing seems to be advancing. The existence of at least one electronic journal, *New Hori-*

*zons in Adult Education,* may be challenging traditional style requirements, but the journal is prospering. In addition, the editorial policy of the Canadian Association for the Study of Adult Education clearly recognizes the place of electronic media in the publication process. The *Canadian Journal for the Study of Adult Education,* which goes to print only once a year, maintains a computer file of articles that is available to its members and to libraries. While only a portion of those in this computer file make it to the printed page, much information can be shared using this technology. Second, computer clearinghouses and data bases, such as that maintained by the Educational Resources Information Center (ERIC), give authors another way to share their work and to access the work of others. According to Adrian (1988, p. 16), "educators writing documents or articles for publication in professional and scholarly journals desire to have their writing read and cited. Today, as a part of achieving this end, publications need to be easily accessible through computerized searching (on-line and CD-ROM) in databases such as ERIC." Thus, technology helps the successful author both in preparing and disseminating a manuscript. Electronic mail, for example, through services such as BITNET can save a great deal of time in correspondence between author and editor.

The potential author can also use networking to inquire about publication possibilities. The new as well as the established author should never hesitate to inquire. The worst one can be told is no, but if one never asks then there may be many missed opportunities. Writers can ask editors if they would be interested in a specific topic and how they might like to see the topic pursued. Van Til (1986, p. 20) advised, "I don't deny that some unsolicited manuscripts are published. But I do urge you to increase your chances of acceptance by adopting the query procedure." Henson (1984) reported that most editors really do not want letters of inquiry, but he suggested using them anyway. Such inquiries can eliminate the effort of submitting a manuscript that would be quickly rejected because it addresses an inappropriate topic for a particular publication or because it has recently been covered by that publication.

One should also ask colleagues for advice on possible ways to get ideas into print. Indeed, practitioners may want to ask a colleague with some experience in publishing to collaborate on an article. Henson (1987, p. 27) pointed out that there are both advantages and disadvantages to collaborating: "collaboration allows a writer to learn from the partner. . . . [But] exercise care when choosing a collaborator; otherwise, what is expected to be an enjoyable experience can turn into a frustrating nightmare."

## Being Realistic

First-time writers need to keep a healthy sense of realism about their efforts to publish. Many published authors start their publication career with reviews. In today's educational world, that means not only reviews of books but also of software, video, and other resources. One's chances for success in publishing may be greatly enhanced by coauthoring articles with a more established writer. Also, new writers, as well as experienced ones, should consider Henson's (1987, p. 28) advice, "A different form of collaboration that can be helpful for the beginning writer is an informal support group that meets periodically to discuss and share ideas for writing."

Most important, no matter how much a rejection hurts, one must remember that every writer receives rejections. There is not one author in this book, nor in most others, who does not have some letters of rejection. According to Markland (1983, p. 139), "anyone who wants to be published must be ready to accept criticism, evaluate it, and use it. Rejections can be turned into lessons if the beginning author will learn from them." Markland also cautions that initial reactions of anger, shock, and insult must be overcome so that "common sense can guide the writer through the criticism to an improvement and a surer evaluation of what has been written." Using the comments in a rejection letter to improve a piece and then resubmitting it are important strategies for successful publication.

Educators of adults who are new at writing may want to consider one of the Educational Resources Information Centers as a first source for publication. The ERIC system for receiving, reviewing, accepting, and disseminating articles is relatively accessible to the first-time writer. It is also a relatively quick process between submission and notification, although once accepted there can be a lengthy wait before the document appears in *Resources in Education* and on microfiche and disk. One clear advantage to ERIC is that once accepted, a document is widely available to educators throughout the nation.

## Conclusion

Writing and professional publication are competitive. However, nonacademicians need not avoid the game because it is challenging. In an information society, professionals should actively engage in the production and dissemination of ideas. To abandon this activity to any one particular group is detrimental to society as a whole. Writing, like giving birth, is primarily the responsibility of one individual; however, help from others is often desirable and necessary. To postpone one's efforts to put into print an idea until after the completion of an advanced degree is not necessary. The importance of professional publication is not its contribution to one's career but rather its contribution to the adult education enterprise. All lifelong learners, whether academician or practitioner, can contribute to this process.

When a writer networks with other professionals, focuses the place, the time, and the message, and understands the audience, the publisher, his or her own style, and what he or she can contribute to the literature, chances for success in publishing are greatly enhanced. All educators of adults need to support the efforts of individuals to contribute to the body of literature in the field. One significant advance for adult and continuing education could come from lessening the competition and increasing the collaboration in publishing professional literature.

### References

Adrian, J. G. "Procedures for Writers in the Field of Education: How to Make Your Publications More Consistently Accessible Within Computerized Information Databases." *New Horizons in Adult Education,* 1988, 2, 16–22.

Apps, J. W. *Improving Your Writing Skills: A Learning Plan for Adults.* Chicago: Follett, 1982.

Atchity, K. J. *A Writer's Time: A Guide to the Creative Process, from Vision Through Revision.* New York: Norton, 1986.

Becker, H. S. *Writing for Social Scientists: How to Start and Finish Your Thesis, Book, or Article.* Chicago: University of Chicago Press, 1986.

Gay, J. T., and Edgil, A. E. "When Your Manuscript Is Rejected." *Nursing & Health Care,* 1990, 10 (8), 459–461.

Henson, K. T. "Writing for Professional Publication: Ways to Increase Your Success." *Phi Delta Kappan,* May 1984, pp. 635–637.

Henson, K. T. *Writing for Professional Publication.* Bloomington, Ind.: Phi Delta Kappa Educational Foundation, 1987.

Markland, M. F. "Taking Criticism—and Using It." *Scholarly Publishing,* February 1983, pp. 139–147.

O'Neill, B. M. "How to Get Published in a Professional Journal." *Journal of Extension,* 1990, 28, 37–38.

Van Til, W. *Writing for Professional Publication.* Needham Heights, Mass.: Allyn & Bacon, 1986.

*Rodney D. Fulton is an active Phi Delta Kappan, a graduate student at Montana State University, an adjunct instructor in the Department of Education, and a research staff member at the College of Nursing, Montana State University, Bozeman.*

*Designing and delivering presentations is a part of practice for adult educators, and its effective management can be achieved through certain clear strategies.*

# Making Effective Presentations: Managing Design and Delivery

*Joan E. Dominick*

Educators of adults have a variety of professional roles, all of which demand a variety of communications skills. Typically, adult educators teach, facilitate, report, plan, explain, and persuade on educational issues before groups of varying audiences. All of these situations demand some form of public presentation. Whether the situation arises out of an invitation to make a formal presentation or a request to make a sudden impromptu talk, today's professional must be comfortable making presentations. This chapter acquaints both the seasoned and the new professional with the necessary skills for designing and delivering a confident presentation.

## What Is a Public Presentation?

Goldhaber (1986) describes presenting as an activity in which the speaker assumes primary responsibility for designing and delivering a message to a group of people. Public presentations are part of the social system model in organizational communication where a balance of information between an organization and the public is sought. Because the majority of adult educators are employed by formal organizations, practitioners need to be able to make efficient and effective presentations both within their organization and externally on behalf of that organization. However, most people feel uncomfortable presenting, perhaps because (1) most have had little experience at it, (2) public speaking is not a skill typically stressed in educational systems, and (3) most people do not enjoy being the center of attention. Whether members of a college class, a continuing education course, or a training seminar, adult participants consistently share the view

NEW DIRECTIONS FOR ADULT AND CONTINUING EDUCATION, no. 51, Fall 1991  © Jossey-Bass Inc., Publishers

that public speaking is a dreaded event. Yet adults are often expected to become eloquent public speakers, regardless of whether or not they have received any instruction in the art of presenting before an audience.

Public speaking is a developed skill, not a talent that one is born with. Thus, the more one delivers presentations, the better one becomes at the process. It helps to realize that the purpose of a presentation is to provide listeners with information on which they can base the best possible decisions concerning local or global issues. Thus, public speaking provides the information necessary to make decisions that provide order in a chaotic or uncertain situation. Informative presentations provide listeners with an information base from which to begin to make decisions. Persuasive presentations provide listeners with evidence to back their decisions. Ceremonial presentations (such as awards banquets) provide listeners with inspiration that the future will be bright based on their present decisions.

## Seven Basic Steps to Making a Presentation

Whether one is delivering an informative, persuasive, or ceremonial presentation, there are seven basic steps to the process: (1) select a topic, (2) formulate a specific purpose, (3) analyze the audience, (4) gather the information, (5) organize the information, (6) rehearse the presentation, and (7) deliver the presentation (Verderber, 1991).

Knowing these seven steps helps one organize the preparation and presentation process. To apply these steps to professional practice, I have developed an approach that focuses on three specific areas:

1. Speaking for an organization: understanding the parameters of the public speaker's accountability
2. Converting stage fright to stage energy: improving physical and vocal delivery by using stage energy effectively
3. Creating the message: analyzing the audience and organizing an effective presentation.

## Representing an Organization

As a professional in adult education, one is often asked to make a presentation on behalf of an organization. In such cases, what is the range of the speaker's accountability? What are the speaker's responsibilities? Basically, one is accountable for all information presented before, during, and after the actual speech delivered. Typically, speakers interact with the audience both before and after the presentation, and it is during this extemporaneous time that most speakers' communication is vulnerable. Even though one might consider whatever one says at these times to be "off the record," a great deal of information is often exchanged, processed, remembered, and repeated.

Because of this, the speaker needs a broader picture of the scope of the presentation. Often speakers think of a presentation as strictly the speech to be delivered. Actually, the presentation begins the moment the speaker steps into the room with the audience. Arriving early, being prepared, and greeting the audience informally before the presentation are some of the methods the speaker can use to begin the interaction with the audience. Through all of this process, the speaker must keep in mind that he or she is functioning as the organization's representative.

Sometimes after a presentation is officially over, there is a question-and-answer period. I refer to this as the "Q-and-A communications gambling period." At this point, many effective speakers become ineffective by mishandling the questions asked. Some tips for handling this portion of the presentation include: (1) be prepared, but don't feel that all questions must be answered immediately; ask for time to research, or ask the audience for assistance; (2) don't let the person asking the question become the speaker; stay in charge; (3) prepare some questions and plant them in the audience; this gives the speaker some control over the direction of the discussion (Bovee and Thill, 1989), and (4) don't be afraid to terminate the question-and-answer period.

Speakers representing an organization should consider documenting their presentations. This protects the speaker in the event the message is inaccurately quoted by the media or misunderstood by the audience. When issues of accountability are at stake, it is better to record the message initially than attempt to recreate from memory what was said.

## Converting Stage Fright to Stage Energy

The term *stage fright* conjures up a variety of reactions, all of them usually negative. Sweating, shaking, fainting, fleeing—all of these actions and impulses can subvert the best-prepared presentation. Every adult educator, faculty member, and graduate student has experienced stage fright at one time or another. The problem is that the term itself becomes a self-fulfilling prophecy for presenters. "Stage fright" sounds negative; therefore, feeling physically and emotionally stressed before a presentation is often assumed to be a negative experience. But these feelings experienced before, during, and after a presentation are perfectly normal. Speakers can learn how to use these feelings as an extra edge provided by nature to combat a stressful situation. In other words, they can learn how to convert stage fright into stage energy. Even great speakers are usually frightened, but they have learned how to make this conversion. What is stage energy? It is an effective force that can make a mediocre speaker into a memorable one.

My experience tells me that stage fright is what holds most people back from presenting in front of groups. This is a tragic loss of wonderful information and ideas that if shared, might assist in the healthy growth of

both individuals and organizations. Freedom of speech is a right for all Americans; however, the skills needed to become a free speaker are not provided for many. Sometimes the educational curriculum does not include public speaking; sometimes people avoid taking a class in public speaking because they don't want to deal with the stress. This lack of formal training contributes to stage fright and its crippling effect on public speakers.

In an effort to minimize stage fright and maximize the stage energy of the speakers in the college classes I facilitate, I ask the students to come to the assistance of nervous speakers through an "emergency group-hug rescue program." When a speaker begins to feel frightened before starting the presentation or during the presentation itself, he or she can ask for a "group hug" from the audience. From their seats, students stretch out their arms toward the speaker, and the speaker is able to relax. The group-hug rescue program works because it acknowledges that it is all right to have stage fright and to admit to having it; it also demonstrates that stage fright does not have to be strictly the speaker's problem—he or she can ask for and get help from the audience. Public speaking is, after all, an interactional activity. Both the speaker and the audience need each other for the success of the event. Consciously developing rapport with the audience not only can help reduce the stage fright of the speaker but it also enhances the value of the audience.

Through my experience as a facilitator of adult education seminars, I have developed a twelve-step program to assist in the conversion of stage fright into stage energy. Predictably, many participants in my classes want to spend most of their time sharing their "war stories" about stage fright. After sharing, we try to develop a management strategy for their fear, and this has become the twelve-step program described in the paragraphs that follow.

**Step One: Combat Mental Jitters.** One way to reduce negative thinking about the upcoming presentation is to shift one's focus to how the audience will benefit from this presentation. Instead of negative "self-talk" such as "I'm boring," "I'm not as good as the previous speaker," "I'm not prepared," speakers should think about ways they can enhance the life of the audience. This process involves conducting an in-depth audience analysis in order to provide the most useful presentation possible. There is no such thing as a boring topic, but there are boring ways to present a topic, and these can be avoided if the speaker focuses on the audience.

**Step Two: Combat Physical Jitters.** Physical reactions to stage fright can consist of sweaty palms, a dry mouth, shaking body parts, out-of-body experiences, and any number of other negative feelings. When I ask people to share these feelings, the lists are long, hilarious, and scary. The point is that we all experience these feelings, and we can all learn to manage them productively. Because public speaking is a stressful event, our bodies meet the challenge by giving us an extra boost of adrenaline. One can harness

this adrenaline by doing relaxation exercises before the presentation. Simple walking, stretching, or yoga exercises will help reduce the physical stress. Speakers should also reduce their caffeine intake, arrive early, and make contact with the audience before the presentation.

**Step Three: Keep a Diary of Stage Fright Events.** Most people notice that there is a pattern to the occurrences of stage fright. One can experience stage fright long before the presentation, immediately before the presentation, during the presentation, or after the presentation. Keeping a diary that records these experiences can help the speaker reflect on and analyze when and how stage fright occurs, and this process can lead to helpful changes. This type of reflective practice is described in detail in Chapter Nine of this volume.

**Step Four: Observe One's Own Public Speaking.** Speakers need to be critical of themselves but not "their own worst critic." When the presentation is recorded on videotape or audio cassette, one usually discovers that all he or she needs is a little presentation polish. This discovery reduces stage fright immensely.

**Step Five: Consider Different Speaking Behaviors.** Speakers should use a manuscript one time and deliver their speeches extemporaneously the next. A variety of nonverbal behaviors, such as walking around and using the arms and hands for emphasis, can be experimented with. Those who typically use the entire body for the presentation should try the reverse, standing behind the podium and relying only on vocal intonations, facial expressions, and eye contact for emphasis. Whatever the speaker's typical style of delivery is, he or she should vary it. This gives the speaker a new focus and challenge and expands his or her repertoire. Any time speakers can shift the focus from themselves to the presentation, they will be taking steps to reduce stage fright.

**Step Six: Image the Speaking Event.** Creating a mental image of the speaking event in advance helps the speaker to practice, reduce stress, and become familiar with the event. The more the speaker can feel at home in the speaking situation, the more control he or she will have over how it goes.

**Step Seven: Practice in the Actual Room of the Scheduled Presentation.** Familiarizing oneself with the presentation's setting will help the speaker feel at home there. A new setting makes most of us nervous, so speakers should "move in" and set up their new "communications home." If this is not possible, speakers should at least visit the setting before the presentation. This reduces the anxiety of the unknown.

**Step Eight: Review Past Speaking Performances.** After the presentation, speakers should ask for feedback from members of the audience concerning all components of the presentation, such as physical and vocal delivery, clarity of presentation, logic of arguments presented, and accurate analysis of audience needs. Audience feedback provides a fairly accurate reac-

tion to the presentation and assists speakers in making improvements for future performances.

**Step Nine: Observe Other Public Speakers.** Every speaker should analyze why others are effective or ineffective speakers. Speakers can also ask others how they manage stage fright. Most people enthusiastically share their "secrets." The process of collecting and analyzing data from other speakers' presentations provides a valuable source of information for one's own repertoire. In addition, reading the speeches of others can provide examples of both speech preparation and speech delivery. The journal entitled *Vital Speeches* provides the complete texts of a variety of speakers across a range of topics and settings, such as education, politics, and religion. *Vital Speeches* can be found at most academic libraries and is an invaluable teaching and learning tool for all types of public speakers, from the novice to the expert.

**Step Ten: Rehearse the Speech.** Practicing the presentation at least five or six times, preferably in front of an honest critic, will enhance the confidence of the speaker and reduce the anxiety of the unknown. If possible, speakers should utilize a videotape recorder to get a sense of how the presentation is progressing. Although no rehearsal will be replicated exactly when the actual event arrives, looking at the delivery and content of the presentation ahead of time helps the speaker to shape the ultimate performance, and knowing that one is well prepared greatly reduces stage fright.

**Step Eleven: Deliver the Presentation.** As the event approaches, speakers can still cancel or delegate the presentation to someone else. But they shouldn't do that; they should show up and deliver the speech. All this preparation should lead to a presentation fueled by positive stage energy. As an additional incentive, speakers should design some reward for themselves after completing a job well done.

**Step Twelve: Update the Public Speaking Diary After the Presentation.** Finally, speakers should update their diary as soon as possible after each presentation. This task not only brings closure to the presentation process but it also helps the speaker to get ready for the next time he or she will present.

After each speech, speakers should acknowledge that preparing for and making the presentation has been quite an accomplishment. The presentation may well have helped, inspired, or solved a problem for at least one person attending, which is, after all, the goal of public speaking.

## Creating the Message

The third area that speakers need to focus on in preparing and delivering a presentation is the creation of the message itself. This is the process of designing the presentation, and it involves two important tasks: analyzing the audience and organizing one's speech.

**Analyzing the Audience.** This process is much like conducting a needs assessment in adult education. If possible, as part of the speaker's preparation, he or she should determine the audience's knowledge of the topic, cohesiveness as a group (are they members of the general public, from the same organization, or all administrators?), general attitude toward the topic (is the topic controversial, or is the audience apathetic toward it?), and level of education (but speakers must not underestimate anyone at any level; some of my most challenging groups have been young children). Speakers should remember that meanings reside in people's perceptions of what is said, not in the words themselves. So speakers need to reduce the amount of jargon used, regardless of the group present, and be prepared for misunderstandings of the message. The language of the presentation should be designed to suit the occasion.

Since the point of a public presentation lies in creating an interaction with the audience, the speaker must consider the audience's needs in all aspects of preparing and presenting the speech. Thus, when presenting, the speaker should constantly read the nonverbal signals from the audience. These signals indicate whether the audience is involved, bored, tired, or confused. If the speaker trusts these signals, he or she can avoid losing the audience by sticking rigidly to the prepared presentation. Some of the most powerful presentations are ones where the speaker stops what was planned and responds to the needs of the audience immediately. In such cases, the audience will not only appreciate the speaker but they will also remember the presentation. Speakers must take risks and keep interacting with the audience.

The following lists provide some tips for dealing with various responses from an audience.

*Friendly Audience: Willing to Support the Speaker's Claims*
1. Make the presentation interesting.
2. Enlist audience members' pride; stimulate them.
3. Don't alienate the audience by overselling them on concepts.
4. Provide the most current information.
5. Work just as hard as one would for a hostile audience.

*Neutral Audience: Undecided or Indifferent Toward the Issue*
1. Establish that there is a reason to be concerned about the issue.
2. Try to find out what has prevented a decision.
3. Explain the issue thoroughly.
4. Be empathic; try to understand the audience's indecision.
5. Focus on only a few aspects of the issue.

*Hostile Audience: Moderately to Radically Against the Issue*
1. Meet the chief objection.

2. Respect the opposition.
3. Use recent evidence.
4. Introduce the controversial solution later in the presentation.
5. Remember that the speaker's job is to provide arguments so that the audience can make accurate decisions relating to the topic.

**Organizing the Presentation.** Whether designing an informative, persuasive, or ceremonial presentation, speakers can follow a basic format to maintain order and ensure a concise presentation. Each presentation has three basic parts: the introduction, the body, and the conclusion. A common formula for the presentation outline is "tell them what you're going to say, then tell them, then tell them what you've just told them." This outline provides enough repetition of the main points of the presentation to increase the odds that the audience will remember them. It also should enhance the clarity of the message and allow for a logical sequencing of the material. Since one goal of a presentation is to help the audience reach a fair decision, then the clearer the material is, the easier it should be for the audience to understand the issues on which they should base that decision. Clear outlines encourage more effective reasoning for the audience.

*Introduction.* The introduction has four parts: attention material, purpose, background information, and a preview of the main points. Attention material is used to gain the interest of the audience. The speaker does not have to open with a joke! Attention material is a quick way of bringing the group to order. A quick story, a quotation, a question are just some of the ways the speaker can gain the attention of the audience. The attention material sets the tone of the presentation, so speakers should make sure it reflects the intended tone. Some speakers open with a joke (and a bad joke, at that), only to deliver a serious fundraising presentation. Don't confuse the audience; rather, pique their interest in the topic with the attention material.

Clearly state the purpose of the presentation. Tell the audience what the topic will be and why it is important. Audiences don't have time to guess the topic. Tell them the topic and proceed with the presentation.

Provide the audience with some background material. This can include definitions, history, or an update on the topic. This allows the audience to share a similar frame of reference.

In the last part of the introduction, the speaker previews the main points to be covered. This acts like an advertisement for the presentation. By telling the audience what will be covered, the speaker provides direction for the presentation.

*Body of the Presentation.* The body of the presentation is divided into its logical components, or main points. One can organize the main points chronologically, topically, spatially, or through comparison and contrast for an informative presentation. For a persuasive presentation, main arguments

can be presented deductively, inductively, or in a problem-solution or cause-and-effect sequence. When delivering a persuasive presentation, speakers should remember to use a combination of logical and emotional main arguments. This approach helps provide a broader picture for the audience. Since we don't understand why people make decisions the way they do, we need to provide a variety of evidence. Regardless of the format, one should highlight the main points by using a numbering or lettering system to help the audience follow the line of reasoning during the presentation. When the speaker has more complicated main points to present, he or she should provide internal summaries; these recap each main point before the speaker moves on to the next one.

Conclusion. Speakers need to develop a strong conclusion for the presentation. The conclusion should review the main points, arguments, or values, and then provide a detailed summary of the presentation. This may seem like a lot of repetition, but after all, the audience is not only hearing the presentation for the first time but they are also making decisions based on its clarity and logic.

## Tips for Managing the Nonverbal Elements of the Presentation

A final area of concern for public speakers is learning how to manage the nonverbal elements of their delivery. Nonverbal communications should complement, not contradict, the verbal ones. The nonverbal aspect of the presentation can easily interfere with the presenter's content. Littlejohn (1989) states that both verbal and nonverbal forms of communication combine to provide an almost limitless variety of messages. Controlling the nonverbal messages is an effective way to enhance a presentation.

Where should I look? How should I stand? What should I do with my hands? Should I walk around during the presentation? How can I manage notes while delivering my presentation? These are some of the endless questions I get from my adult students as we try to improve their physical delivery. The funniest yet most poignant comment concerning this topic was made recently by a student in my college class. After delivering a ceremonial speech in my class, this young man turned to me and said, "If I could only paint eyeballs on my eyelids, I would have it made as a public speaker!" Why? I inquired. "Well, then I could look at my audience, read from my notes, and generally feel in control." We can't paint eyeballs on our eyelids, but I can make a few suggestions that might relieve the urge to do so.

Maintaining Eye Contact. Good physical delivery consists of maintaining eye contact with the audience, using one's hands for emphasis, moving when appropriate, maintaining good posture, and having appropriate facial expressions during the presentation. Of these elements, main-

taining eye contact with the audience seems to be the largest problem for most public speakers. Establishing and maintaining eye contact helps the speaker develop a relationship with audience members, inviting them to listen, and helps reduce the speaker's fears by showing him or her that the audience is on his or her side.

How can the speaker establish and maintain eye contact with the audience?

*Arrive Early for the Presentation.* Speakers should look for receptive faces and smile or greet them. In this way, the speaker can discover a few friendly faces to look at during the presentation, and he or she will have begun to build a relationship with the audience.

*Divide the Audience into Manageable Sections for Viewing.* The speaker should mentally divide the audience into sections, such as front, middle, and rear, or right, middle, and left. Then, while speaking, he or she can try to spend time looking directly at each one of the sections. Each audience member should feel that the speaker has looked at him or her at least once during the presentation. This practice gives the speaker more control and makes the audience pay more attention. Once a speaker has made eye contact with a member of the audience, it becomes difficult for the audience member to look away. For the same reason, the speaker should not look for too long at any one person, as this can make that person feel trapped.

Speakers want a relationship with the audience; maintaining eye contact is critical to developing that relationship. If the audience is engaged in eye contact with the speaker, they are more likely to listen actively to him or her.

*Try Speaking Extemporaneously.* Speakers should write a detailed outline and refer to it only when necessary. Notes can be written on a cue card the size of the podium and divided into three columns: introduction, body, and conclusion. The columns should be color coded so that the speaker can refer quickly to them without losing eye contact with the audience for any length of time. If one must speak from a manuscript, it should be printed in large type, which is quite easy to do with today's word processors and copier machines. The presenter can indicate on the manuscript where to take natural breaks and establish eye contact with the audience. Using a manuscript introduces another set of questions for public speakers, including, Should I hold the manuscript? Should I try to use my hands while reading? If one is reading from a manuscript, the physical aspect of the delivery will usually consist of maintaining eye contact and using some occasional hand movements. Speakers should not hold the manuscript throughout the entire presentation, as this can encourage them simply to read rather than present.

**Using Hand Movements.** What to do with one's hands during a presentation could be called the plague of public speakers. I was taught to glue them to my sides as if it were shameful to show one's palms during a

presentation. Hand movements, however, can provide emphasis, punctuation, and drama during a presentation. I once witnessed a speaker in a basic public speaking class walk off with a portable podium after completing a speech. The speaker had gripped the podium so tightly during the performance that his hands had fused with the podium. The speaker was just as surprised as the audience.

To prevent such mishaps, I offer four tips for using one's hands productively during a presentation. First, speakers should remember that there is almost no wrong hand movement. Thus, they should try to vary their hand movements occasionally. On the other hand, hand movements are not the central focus of the presentation; they are only for emphasis and should not overpower the presentation. Second, speakers should use their hands to make a point visually. This is called "iconic gesturing." The hands complement the message. Third, speakers can use their hands to demonstrate visual aids. Fourth, if one does not want to use hand movements during the presentation, the hands can be placed on the podium. But speakers should not be tempted to cling to note cards or the podium itself. Using one large cue card that rests on the podium or desk, rather than a set of small note cards, frees the speaker's hands and adds a more relaxed appearance to the speaker's performance.

**Using Visual Aids.** Visual aids provide a natural way to use one's hands during a presentation. Typically, speakers tend to use charts, slides, transparencies, videos, flip charts, objects, and handouts to clarify various points or arguments in the presentation. Whatever visual aid is used, speakers should ensure it does not upstage them. Visual aids that can upstage the speaker include those that are hard to read, contain errors, are overcrowded with information and don't relate to the topic. Speakers should keep the visual aid simple, rehearse with it, and then be sure to use it during the presentation. Visual aids that are not used yet are visible to the audience become a distraction.

Bovee and Thill (1989) suggest that handouts should be used for smaller audiences (those of under a hundred people). When using several handouts, speakers can try color coding rather than numbering them. Audiences are appreciative because they do not have to search for the number and title of the handout. Color coding handouts saves time and energy and reduces audience distraction. And the goal of visual aids is enhancement, not distraction.

**Managing Vocal Delivery.** Some tips on improving vocal delivery include the following: (1) speak loudly, (2) sound enthusiastic, (3) pronounce words correctly, (4) speak moderately fast, and (5) if using a microphone, make sure it works. The audience must be able to hear the presentation. They will yell at the speaker if they cannot hear, and since this is usually upsetting, speakers should avoid as many vocal delivery problems as possible.

## Conclusion

The following steps to public speaking have been offered as a guide for presenters: (1) maintain a sense of one's accountability, (2) manage stage energy, (3) analyze the audience, (4) design a detailed outline, and (5) work on one's physical delivery. These are the basic ingredients for designing and delivering an effective presentation. Making public presentations is one of the responsibilities of professional practice. The insights provided here can help make the speaker's preparation efficient and can help ensure that effective communication occurs.

## References

Bovee, C. L., and Thill, J. V. *Business Communication Today.* New York: Random House, 1989.

Goldhaber, G. M. *Organizational Communication.* (3rd ed.) Dubuque, Iowa: Brown, 1986.

Littlejohn, S. W. *Theories of Human Communication.* Belmont, Calif.: Wadsworth, 1989.

Verderber, R. *Essentials of Persuasive Speaking: Theory and Contexts.* Belmont, Calif.: Wadsworth, 1991.

*Joan E. Dominick is assistant professor of communications at Kennesaw State College, Marietta, Georgia.*

*Serving as a leader in a volunteer-based professional association requires a special combination of skills, talent, and understanding.*

# Leadership Through Professional Associations

*Elaine Shelton, W. Franklin Spikes*

Leadership is a frequently studied, often discussed, and somewhat elusive concept. Today's popular and scholarly presses regularly contain articles that examine leadership styles, analyze leadership traits, or describe individuals who exhibit model leadership behaviors. While there is frequent disagreement among those who study leadership as to what characteristics are common to today's leaders, there is almost universal agreement that there is no one best way to achieve positions of leadership in modern society. Perhaps these positions are attained by being in the "right place at the right time," having influential friends and family members, or raising a great deal of money, or perhaps just working hard throughout a career will permit one to rise to a position of influence and leadership. The field of adult and continuing education is no different from others when it comes to developing leaders. Opportunities of all sorts abound.

Historically, professional associations have provided excellent ways for educators of adults to increase their knowledge, develop new skills, and expand leadership competencies. Regional conferences, professional journals and books, and membership and participation on statewide and national governing boards and committees are some of the many mechanisms that most associations provide for developing emerging volunteer leaders.

Unfortunately, educators often perceive the process of achieving positions of leadership in professional associations as one that is either cloaked in secrecy or fraught with political infighting. In certain instances, politics and unclear policies and practices do hinder the full participation and development of potential leaders, but this is not always the case. Thus, this

NEW DIRECTIONS FOR ADULT AND CONTINUING EDUCATION, no. 51, Fall 1991 © Jossey-Bass Inc., Publishers

chapter focuses on how educators of adults can use professional associations to increase their individual leadership skills and how they can participate more fully in the governance of these groups.

The chapter discusses the practical realities of professional association leadership. It begins with a brief look at the range of associations in the adult and continuing education field; then the emphasis shifts to suggestions about how one can maximize one's individual leadership experiences within an association. Included here is a discussion of the specific skills that successful association leaders develop.

## Professional Associations in Adult and Continuing Education

Over the years, the literature has addressed various issues related to professional associations. Among the more recent of these works are Brockett (1989) and Spikes (1989). The former is a comprehensive discussion of professional associations in the field of adult and continuing education; it includes information about functions and types of professional associations and possible future activities of these groups. Spikes's work examines some of the historical roots of professional associations and discusses the viability of such organizations in light of today's changing economic climate.

Adult educators have a long and "rich history of banding together at the local, regional, and national levels to form groups, councils, and associations that serve specific or more general needs of the field" (Spikes, 1989, p. 64). In 1915 the National University Extension Association (NUEA) was formed. With the assistance of the Carnegie Corporation, the American Association for Adult Education (AAAE) was then founded in 1926. After that, a variety of other national bodies were formed, including the American Society for Training and Development (ASTD); the National Association for Public Continuing Adult Education (NAPCAE); the Adult Education Association of the United States (AEA/USA); and the American Association for Adult and Continuing Education (AAACE), which consolidated AEA/USA and NAPCAE into one national organization in 1982. These groups, however, represent only the tip of the association iceberg. A number of years ago, Knowles (1977) identified more than ninety associations or organizations with interests in the field of adult and continuing education. It is reasonable to assume that with the continuing specialization in the field, this number has increased since Knowles's work was published. An example of a new association with a specific area of interest is the National Association for Adults with Special Learning Needs (NAASLN). Like many professional groups today, NAASLN has identified a specific clientele on which to focus its energies and the interests of its members.

The literature as well as practice reveals that many purposes exist for professional associations. When viewed from the most global perspective,

however, professional associations have been seen as serving "one of two primary roles: unification of the field or meeting the specialized needs of the field" (Brockett, 1989, p. 115). To accomplish these goals, professional associations are often organized around geographical boundaries. Thus, we have local, state, regional, provincial, national, or international groups that operate within our field. Similarly, we have organizations that focus on special interests, like NAASLN, or that have a more broadly based constituency, such as AAACE.

Smith, Eyre, and Miller (1982) have suggested another way to categorize professional associations: by the type of membership that is served. Using this system, they identified three types: (1) associations of associations—that is, groups that have other associations as members; (2) institutionally based associations, such as the National University Continuing Education Association (NUCEA), which can be joined only by institutions; and (3) associations such as AAACE that provide services to individual members.

Clearly, there are many professional associations that serve the adult education field. Each of us needs to decide how to allocate our limited time and financial resources so that we can get the most from our involvement in these groups.

## Getting Involved in Professional Associations

Professional associations are an invaluable resource for professional development. One can benefit from merely joining an association, reading its publications, and perhaps attending the annual conference. But, more important, associations can be a place where one can make an active contribution. In Chapters Five and Six, Fulton and Dominick discuss strategies to use in writing for publication and delivering professional presentations. Associations offer an outlet for both of these activities.

However, the greatest benefits of membership can probably be gained by taking an active leadership role in the organization. For many individuals, especially new members, this can be an intimidating thought. But it doesn't need to be. What better way is there to learn about an association than by becoming involved in some aspect of its operation? The structure of most associations offers opportunities to get involved in a wide range of ways, from participation in special interest groups to association-wide leadership.

Since most, if not all, association activities typically operate on a volunteer basis, there is always a need for new individuals to play a role. Indeed, the success and survival of professional associations depend on the involvement of committed individuals. The best advice we can offer here, especially to those who are new to the field or to their organization, is to think about where one can best contribute, and then jump in. The

remainder of this chapter addresses some of the specific leadership skills and issues of voluntary organization management that have been confronted by the authors of this chapter during their terms as leaders in AAACE and through their service to several of the other types of professional associations described in the previous section.

## Skills Gained Through Professional Association Leadership

Membership in professional associations can and often does lead to the development or enhancement of leadership skills. Such skills are both overt and covert, to greater and lesser degrees. Some of the more overt skills and knowledge developed through association leadership relate to association business, specifically in the areas of budgeting, staffing, publishing, marketing, and conference planning or managing.

**Budgeting.** For all but those educators who are responsible for fiscal planning and management as part of their jobs, budgeting often seems like one of the more profoundly intimidating aspects of association business. This is even more true for associations composed of voluntary boards of directors. Ignorance of or lack of interest in the financial affairs of the professional association is not acceptable if one is to be taken seriously as an association leader. Because each board member has fiduciary responsibility for the financial health or illness of the association, it is incumbent on each to take an active role in understanding, questioning, tracking, and acting on all fiscal matters that have an impact on the association.

**Staffing.** Leaders of professional associations are privy to the often bumpy road of staff composition, strengths, weaknesses, and interpersonal relations. By watching the ways the chief executive officer (CEO) handles various situations (such as variable productivity and competence levels, grievances, delegation, authority, personality conflicts, and so on), lower-level leaders can learn by example—to emulate, if the CEO serves as a good example, or to avoid, if the example is a poor one. By asking themselves what decisions they would make under similar circumstances, leaders can help prepare themselves for future leadership roles and responsibilities. The adage is "learn from one's mistakes," but this can reasonably be expanded to include learning from both the mistakes and the successes of others.

**Publishing.** Professional associations are excellent places in which to learn the "ins and outs" of publishing. Most professional associations publish scholarly journals that focus on research and theory, practitioner magazines that relate research to practice, practical special interest pamphlets that describe "how to do the job better," and association newsletters. Interested association leaders are able to receive a liberal education in conceptualizing, designing, producing, pricing, marketing, and disseminating such

publications. This knowledge can prove highly transferable to other job tasks and responsibilities.

**Marketing.** Receptive leaders of professional associations receive valuable working knowledge and skills not only in marketing the publications just mentioned but also in marketing membership in the association. All the direct targeted mailings in the world cannot hold a candle to the effectiveness of an individual being asked personally by an association leader to join the group. Marketing also extends to the proactive advertising of the association's conferences.

**Conference Planning and Managing.** The leader of a professional association often has direct (and certainly indirect) input into the content and format of the association's conferences. Even if such involvement is not always direct, leaders who have strong feelings about some aspect of the conference are often able to shape it to fit their objectives.

This recognition—that association leaders are often in a position to facilitate the accomplishment of goals and to guide and affect desired change through conference agendas, publication plans, committees, task forces, and so forth—provides a good segue into a discussion of some of the more covert (yet still extremely valuable) skills that association leaders often gain through their participation.

**Organizational Skills.** The fact that leadership in a professional association often has time parameters is a mixed blessing. On the negative side, one is often frustrated and disappointed to realize how relatively little can be accomplished (particularly with voluntary working groups) during the leader's term of office. On the positive side, this fact helps increase the leader's skills in organizing and managing time, prioritizing and compromising, identifying dependable and competent workers, and delegating some of the work load to them.

**Decision-Making and Problem-Solving Skills.** Leaders of professional associations are constantly called on to exercise their decision-making and problem-solving skills. If the saying "use it or lose it" is true, association leaders should have nothing to fear! Some of the decisions with which leaders of professional associations are faced force the prioritizing and compromising to which we just referred. Just as important as the decision about what to accomplish is the decision about how best to accomplish it. This fact, sometimes lost on association leaders, leads to a discussion of the next set of skills.

**Interpersonal Relations Skills.** Often, particularly in a professional association made up of volunteer workers, how leaders decide to present an issue or charge a committee determines whether or not the task will be accomplished and the goal reached. The ability to make those persons with whom the leader is working feel that they are an integral part of decision making helps to instill a sense of ownership in decisions and policies.

**Communications Skills.** Effective communications skills in both writing and speaking are critically important for association leaders. It could be said that in order to be chosen for a professional association leadership position, one must possess at least rudimentary skills in communicating with others. On the other hand, once one attains a position of leadership, such skills are honed and fine-tuned. Again, how one communicates is often just as important, if not even more important, than what is being communicated.

## Developing Leadership Skills Through Professional Association Networks

The development or enhancement of all these skills often leads to the development of yet another aspect of association leadership: that of mentoring.

Effective leaders' skills are often highly visible to members who, in turn, seek the leaders out for advice and counsel. Unselfish leaders will be not only flattered by this obvious show of respect and confidence from peers but also generous in sharing their knowledge. The mentoring process, whether formal or (as is more often the case) informal, builds the self-confidence of both mentor and advisee. Increased self-confidence, in fact, is an important offshoot of enhanced skill levels.

Mentoring is one aspect of another element of association membership—an element that represents, in fact, one of the most valued skills honed through association leadership. This skill is networking. As valuable as the knowledge gained through association publications, conferences, and seminars, networking opportunities are typically one of the major reasons given for joining a professional association in the first place, for remaining in the association, and for attending its conferences. When almost two thousand people, members and nonmembers, gather in one city for a period of two and a half to three days, incomparable networking opportunities exist. The frenetic pace of conference attendees, particularly the leaders, makes it difficult to pin some individuals down for even informal chat, but it is by no means impossible. A telephone call prior to the conference to those persons with whom one most desires to talk can serve to arrange a mutually convenient meeting time and place and saves the arduous task of locating these people at the conference via messages left at their hotel or on conference message boards. Another good way to network with persons at conferences is to find out if and when they are presenting, attend their session, and then stay to speak with them after the session, exchange business cards, and so on.

Since financial and time constraints sometimes proscribe conference attendance, networking can be facilitated via written communications or by telephone. This is particularly appropriate if one wants to follow up on

an article written in one of the association's publications. While often not as satisfactory as face-to-face meetings, these methods have, in many cases, begun a "pen-pal" or even a mentoring relationship that can blossom into the more desired face-to-face communications later.

In any form, networking is an avenue to becoming an association leader as well as a means of nurturing close relationships with those persons whose professional skills and knowledge or personal friendship one might wish to maintain.

By cultivating just such networking opportunities, one of the authors of this chapter rose from grass-roots project director to an active member of one of AAACE's interest units and then from committee member to chair of that unit; next the author was elected to the board of directors of the division under which the unit fell, then elected as director-at-large, and finally was chosen president-elect of the association. The nine years that these leadership positions covered afforded an ever-increasing breadth of responsibility and potential for affecting the directions the association took, and all of these positions were a direct result of effectively networking with and gaining the respect of colleagues around North America. Many of these networking opportunities arose from faithful attendance and presentation at yearly conferences of the professional association and of two of its special interest units. Over the years, such networking among colleagues developed the familiarity, respect, and trust necessary for the membership to elect each of the chapter authors to the highest leadership position in the association.

Skills gained through participation in a professional association can sometimes be directly transferable to one's actual job responsibilities. The following is an example of how this transferability has worked since the time that one of the authors served as a director-at-large in AAACE.

The responsibilities of a director-at-large are determined by assignments given by the association's president. In this case, the assignment to the author during her term as director-at-large was to develop the policies and procedures for the association's speaker's bureau. Such a bureau allowed AAACE affiliates to avail themselves of the services of expert speakers on the basis of actual costs only. Some five years later, this experience has translated directly into the development and coordination of a literacy speaker's bureau in the city in which the author now resides.

## Conclusion

We have primarily addressed the positive elements of leadership in professional associations. Here and there we have touched on some of the more negative, frustrating aspects of leadership. It is not a coincidence that when the negative aspects have been addressed, more often than not they have been couched in terms that reveal a positive side, too. In other words, even the negative realities of leadership can lead to the acquisition of positive skills. For example, the frustration with the sometimes too deliberate speed and indecision with which committees operate can be turned into increased tolerance for ambiguity. The realization of how relatively little can actually be accomplished in a short term of leadership, especially by volunteer workers, can be turned around from dampened idealism to heightened realism. Indeed, a fellow professional association leader was particularly struck by one of the authors characterizing her term as president of AAACE as a year of "reality therapy." And last, the prodigious amounts of time and energy consumed in both running for and serving in leadership capacities in professional associations clearly can be seen to lead to increased delegation and management skills. The bottom line is that leadership in professional associations, while often frustrating, is more than amply compensated for by being challenging, exciting, and one of the most highly rewarding and skill-building activities in which the two authors of this chapter have had the privilege to be engaged. We recommend the pursuit of leadership in professional associations to the readers of this chapter as a remarkable way to broaden your horizons.

## References

Brockett, R. G. "Professional Associations in Adult and Continuing Education." In S. B. Merriam and P. M. Cunningham (eds.), *Handbook of Adult and Continuing Education*. San Francisco: Jossey-Bass, 1989.

Knowles, M. S. *A History of the Adult Education Movement in the United States.* (Rev. ed.) Malabar, Fla.: Krieger, 1977.

Smith, W. S., Eyre, G. A., and Miller, J. W. "Join Your Professional Organizations." In C. Kelvins (ed.), *Materials and Methods in Adult and Continuing Education*. Los Angeles: Kelvins Publications, 1982.

Spikes, W. F. "Developing Our Own Professional Associations and Building Bridges to Others." In B. A. Quigley (ed.), *Fulfilling the Promise of Adult and Continuing Education*. New Directions for Continuing Education, no. 44. San Francisco: Jossey-Bass, 1989.

*Elaine Shelton is president of Shelton Associates and a former president of the American Association for Adult and Continuing Education.*

*W. Franklin Spikes is professor and chair of the Department of Adult and Continuing Education at Kansas State University, and he is president of the American Association for Adult and Continuing Education for 1991–92.*

*Graduate school can be a place for building competencies and building the "vita"—two dimensions of successful professional development.*

# Graduate Study as Professional Development

*Catherine P. Zeph*

Entering graduate school was a decision I made after hearing more than a few people who managed continuing education centers say to me, "We would love to hire you, but you need a master's degree." Even though I had the skills, the temperament, and the basic smarts to catch on to what a beginning job in continuing education required, I still was told I needed a degree in the field. Some people encouraged me to pursue a master's degree in counseling; after some inquiries and reflection, I decided on a master's in adult education. I was not sure why, but I knew that I did not want to study counseling for fear that that would be all I could do when I graduated.

There it is, the magic word: graduated. All students live for the glorious feeling of having finished school. Graduate students are in school primarily because academic degrees are the ticket for admittance into the professional world of work, at least in our American society. But there is more to be gained from this advanced schooling than just the degree. This chapter, using both scholarly and personal reflection, discusses how the experiences of graduate school can contribute to a student's professional development in the field of adult education.

## Graduate Study in Adult Education

Graduate school exists for the purposes of professional development. To graduate from a degree program certifies that an individual has learned a body of knowledge, possesses certain skills, and is qualified to practice in a chosen profession; completion of graduate school is often thought of as a major step in the professionalization process. Due to the seemingly ubiquitous nature of the adult education field and the ever-growing need for professional adult educators, graduate students in adult education may be faced with many choices in terms of how to pursue their professional interests. Unlike other graduate or professional programs where students follow a prescribed course of study, adult education students often determine their own course work, initiate their own internships, and select their own research topics based on individual interests and needs. This is largely due to the wide range of interests, experiences, and ages of students who enroll in adult education graduate programs.

**Literature on the Formal Training of Adult Educators.** The formal training of adult educators has been the subject of much discussion in the literature, from the beginnings of the discipline to the present day. Brookfield (1988) has provided an excellent anthology on this subject, comprised of noteworthy articles that reflect on the history and framework of graduate training in the field of adult education. Along with Brookfield's collection, each edition of the adult education handbooks, published periodically since 1936, provides information on graduate training. The most recent handbook, for example, contains an excellent overview of graduate training by Galbraith and Zelenak (1989). Every so often, issues of *Lifelong Learning* and *Adult Learning* have provided a graduate student's perspective on his or her experiences (Fingeret, 1983; Lewis, 1983; Pittman, 1989) or a report or discussion on the state of graduate preparation for those studying adult education (Dowling and Sheehan, 1982; Gschwender, 1982; Bruce, Maxwell, and Galvin, 1986; Weaver and Kowalski, 1987). Increased discussion has appeared recently in the literature relative to professional development for academicians (for example, Schuster, Wheeler, and Associates, 1990). Since there is so much that one can peruse and since space is limited, I will focus here on the characteristics of adult education students and on a few issues of concern regarding graduate training for adult educators. Then I will describe ways in which students can gain experiences that contribute to their professional development.

**Characteristics of Students.** Thirty-five years ago Houle (1956, p. 135) wrote of how most students in adult education enter graduate school by "'the back door'; the comment is made so often as to raise the speculation that there is no front door." This is still the rule rather than the exception. Almost always, colleagues in my adult education courses were between thirty and sixty years old, employed full time, raising families, and pursuing their studies on a part-time basis. They entered degree programs because of a need to understand their work, to promote themselves from within their organization, or in rare cases like my own, to enter into a new career. I have studied with people working in adult education from all arenas of life: military, religious, corporate training and development, social work, nursing, community organizations, counseling, literacy, public education, cooperative extension, and higher education. Together we have shared and learned from each other about our varied contributions to the adult and continuing education field.

**Issues Concerning Graduate Study in Adult Education.** Merriam (1985) lists three issues concerning the professional preparation of adult educators. These issues are addressed throughout the literature, and they have had an impact on my own experience.

The first is a lack of common identity. As pointed out in my description of fellow students, people enter the field of adult education with a variety of other professional allegiances. Those involved in adult education tend to identify themselves in terms of what their content area is (alcohol and drug education or religious education, for example), of what they do on a daily basis (program developer or administrator), or of where they work (cooperative extension or hospital). Rarely do people define themselves solely as adult educators. I have found this particular issue tested time and again at social functions. Introductions to others always include the naming of one's particular career or employer. People understand "lawyer," "accountant," and "doctor"; rarely do they understand "adult educator." Along with or instead of "adult educator," I've had to say, "I work with the Cooperative Extension Service," "I plan and administrate programs," or "I work with county agents to meet their programming needs." Adult education is a profession (a point also of frequent debate) that continually demands explanation, and each person's explanation is different. This identity issue was discussed by Brockett in Chapter One of this volume.

The second issue identified by Merriam is a lack of career structure. People receive adult education degrees at different times in their lives and for different reasons. In addition, depending on one's particular needs or aspirations, different academic training and interests are pursued. Those wanting a faculty career may obtain a graduate assistantship; those wanting more practical application may pursue practicums or internships. Often individuals are already trained in another content area or discipline and feel they are taking a "step back" by going to graduate school in order to obtain professional knowledge and training in the field of adult and continuing education.

The third issue is the lack of evidence that training makes a difference. The fact that graduating from an adult education program does not make one necessarily a better adult educator has been discussed frequently in the literature. Duke (1989, p. 369) states that "it is frequently asserted that good adult educators are born (or matured by experience) rather than produced by formal training and that many of the essential qualities and even skills are difficult or impossible to teach." Graduate school has provided me with a knowledge of the literature on adult education and the societal problems it attempts to address, but my actual training in how adult education "happens" has taken place away from the classroom. Working with local community groups, individuals, colleagues, and professional audiences has given me the confidence and practice needed to mature into a practitioner of adult education. Graduate school has given me the space and time to reflect on questions of practice and to think and write in the "professional" ways of the field.

**Building Competencies and Building the "Vita."** What, then, is professional development for graduate students in the field of adult education? Professional development is often thought of as occurring after a student has graduated—that is, when he or she is a "professional" and no longer considered a student. But the numerous roles that individuals play do interrelate and cannot be separated. As previously discussed, most students in adult education are studying part time and are already holding professional positions. Whether one wants to pursue an academic or practitioner track of study, one can find opportunities in school to develop one's competencies and credibility for future employment. Professional development for students of adult education, then, is the practice of competencies and the development of credibility in order to secure later employment as an adult educator. What I would like to propose is that graduate school is a place for both building competencies and building the "vita."

Because graduate training in adult education is so diverse and responds to the needs of each particular student, one cannot look to graduate school as a place where all the expertise that is needed for professional work can be gained. Rather, what graduate school can provide is an opportunity for professional networking, for some fine-tuning of skills, and for beginning to make various kinds of contributions to the field. By taking advantage of these opportunities, graduate students can engage in activities that contribute to their curriculum vitae ("vita" or résumé). Gradually, these different experiences build a confidence and credibility that contribute to and enrich the student's professional development. The building of competencies and building of the vita are each processes and products that blend together to create the thing called professional development.

## Professional Development Activities

Recently, the Commission of Professors of Adult Education published the *Standards for Graduate Programs in Adult Education* (Commission of Professors of Adult Education, n.d.). At its conclusion, under the heading of "Scholarship," this publication provides a list of the "outcomes of a high-quality graduate program." The list includes such outcomes as publications in refereed journals, publications of books and reports, contributions to conferences, exchanges (including international ones) between programs, service to the field and profession, and the placement and performance of program alumni. These outcomes contribute to the overall professional development of any individual, no matter what their field of work. Even before seeing this list, I had developed, based on my own experiences, a similar set of activities that can contribute to a student's professional development. It is my list that I wish to share in the paragraphs that follow.

**Professional Associations and Leadership.** Opportunities abound for students in professional associations. Attending conferences, taking on leadership roles, presenting papers at meetings, or publishing articles in association journals provide much in the way of professional development. Brockett (1989) gives an overview of professional associations within the field of adult and continuing education; all associations encourage students to become involved. Shelton and Spikes, in Chapter Seven of this volume, also discuss the role of associations in professional development. The following are some ways in which students can benefit from such involvement.

Attending national conferences is a multifaceted opportunity for professional development. The energy created by the presence of so many people, the ideas generated and shared, the exhibits, special events, and presentations can be at times overwhelming but often exhilarating. By placing themselves in a different environment, students open themselves up to new ideas and people in a way that might not be possible on the home campus. In addition, a different location encourages learning about a different part of the country, which can assist in later job-hunting efforts or just in understanding better a certain location.

Prior to the annual American Association for Adult and Continuing Education (AAACE) meeting, the Commission of Professors hold their annual meeting, and students as well as practitioners are welcome to attend. This is a unique opportunity to meet and mingle with those who do research in the field and who author many of the publications found in the professional literature. For me, meeting these "faces and names" of the field—those who publish or lead well-known programs—has been important in my professional development. It has made me realize that their reputation has been built slowly, rather than sprung up overnight. Whether they are well-known authors and practitioners or lesser-known colleagues and students, I have gained a real education from talking over and sharing ideas and experiences with them at conferences. Learning that other students elsewhere are going through the same graduate school syndromes can be a real morale booster, and contacts made at one conference can bloom into collegial relationships that grow stronger with each professional meeting. To know others are doing the same work, but miles apart, can be exhilarating.

At the Adult Education Research Conference (a smaller research-oriented conference held each spring), students also have the opportunity to meet on a more collegial basis the professors of adult education. Here research ideas are presented and can be discussed in a smaller, more informal setting than at the larger national AAACE conference. Students are encouraged to submit proposals for poster sessions and research papers, and their ideas are given equal attention as those of professors. Papers that are accepted are published in a book of proceedings, and students are encouraged to apply for the Graduate Student Award, which recognizes the outstanding student paper for the conference.

The National University Continuing Education Association (NUCEA) and the Association for Continuing Higher Education are associations of continuing educators working in university settings. Both hold large national meetings, as well as smaller regional and divisional meetings. Some of their meetings offer awards for papers or research; a colleague of mine received an award for her dissertation research at a regional NUCEA conference. The American Society for Training and Development (ASTD) is primarily for those who work as trainers and human resource personnel in the corporate world. They, too, hold yearly conferences and invite students to attend and submit presentation proposals. ASTD has local chapters where students can network, gaining job information and sharing interests within a particular metropolitan area or region.

While many think they need to wait until they are well known before assuming leadership roles, this is not the case for graduate students. For example, at my first national AAACE conference, I decided to go to the graduate student unit meeting. There I met a small group of students, all of whom were holding various leadership positions and were looking for new recruits. I left the meeting as the new editor of the unit's newsletter, while a colleague at my same institution was named president. We worked well over the next year, as the two of us were able to collect and disseminate information together. This was an ideal thing to do, for we learned quickly how the association worked and met others in leadership roles. Students are respected in AAACE, and it is not at all difficult to become involved.

Leadership positions in local, state, or regional associations are also possible. Working with those close to home provides an excellent means of establishing networks among current students, faculty, alumni, and professionals, and these people can later assist the graduate in obtaining employment. Whether one organizes a faculty-student retreat, serves on a committee, or edits a local newsletter, all of these experiences contribute to the vita. Also, the individuals that one interacts with on a regular basis can provide a support system while in graduate school. Only those who share in the student's experiences know what is being undertaken and the energy required to achieve the degree. A leadership role, no matter how big or small, is a way to develop skills, build the vita, and meet others who can be of support.

**Presentations and Publications.** Students do not have to wait until they are an "expert" at something to make a presentation at a conference. In fact, graduate school is the perfect time to try out one's presentation skills. Almost any topic, whether it be a successful program or an idea from a research paper, will be of interest to at least a few others. When writing presentation proposals, stay within the conference guidelines for writing and relevance to the overall theme. Communicate ideas clearly with the intended audience in mind, and an acceptance letter may follow. For a further discussion on presentations, see Chapter Six in this volume.

As a student, publishing articles can be a difficult thing to do. It is enough just to write papers for a class or to be working on a thesis or dissertation. But with motivation and diligence, it can be done. Journals with a more practitioner-based audience may be easier to write for, as personal experiences can be used to tell a story. Papers from classes and, later, from the thesis or dissertation can be fashioned into a publication. Look for opportunities to write, even if it is in a newsletter. More important, as a student, be open to opportunities and encouragement from others. Almost all of my writing, including this chapter, has been at the invitation or encouragement from others. Chapter Five in this volume provides a detailed discussion on publishing.

**Assistantships.** Assistantships are valuable experiences for professional development. They typically take the form of teaching, research, or administrative assistantships. Teaching assistantships allow students to teach various courses in an academic department, either alone or with professors or other students. This is an especially good opportunity for those contemplating an academic career. Not only does the assistantship provide actual practice in teaching in front of a class but it also helps develop confidence and expertise in all the other things that teaching requires: knowledge of a subject matter, relationships with students, and making professional judgments on students' efforts and material learned.

Research or administrative assistantships are great for those who may want to pursue a more practitioner-oriented or an administrative career or for those who may want general exposure to the culture of an academic department. Tasks performed can be varied and assigned as needed. My more glamorous research assistantships included assisting with the editing and publishing of a newsletter, editing and proofing various articles and book manuscripts, writing a conference proposal, and helping to write an article. Not-so-glamorous jobs included answering the telephone, searching for and dropping off books at the library, and licking envelopes and stamps—all in a day's work, and all essential to the running of the department.

**Internships and Practicums.** Internships and practicums allow the student to intern and practice within the work world of adult education, whether in business, at a continuing education organization, or at a university. No matter what the setting, these experiences allow the student to try out skills, make professional contacts, and integrate what he or she is learning in the field with what is being learned in the classroom. These are good experiences for exposure both to other practitioners and to a particular component of adult education. The short-term experiences of practicums and internships often give students flexibility. If an initial experience sparks a real interest, the student may be able to negotiate to spend more time in the internship. Or if a student finds that he or she really does not like the job, knowing that it is a short-term experience may assist in enduring the initial commitment and offer an opportunity to reflect on why the experience was not enjoyable.

**Classes.** Attending classes can stimulate and provide for some professional development. Within the relative safety of a classroom, students can learn how to field challenges in a professional manner. Writing, thinking, debating, listening, speaking, and presentation skills can all be sharpened as students and professors interact with each other. Professors and classmates can also be observed for their teaching and learning styles, as can those of any guest lecturer. Group assignments are often the norm in adult education classes; these assist in sharpening the collaboration and teamwork skills that are needed in adult education work. Current issues and trends in adult education can be examined in a heightened way that may not be available elsewhere. Research papers can be the source of ideas for presentations and publications, while papers from other students and any handouts, including bibliographies and references, can be the start of a professional library. Although the course work in any program can be tiring, it does offer time in which to pursue topics of professional interest and a place where students can share ideas with others who hold similar interests.

**Use of the Library.** Along with attending classes, visiting and even "living" in the library is a major requirement of graduate school. While library research may not always be fun, it is a way to become intimately acquainted with the literature of the field and with the various resources available to researchers. I have heard professors say that graduate students know the literature better than anyone, and I believe this is true. Graduate students are continually immersing themselves in the literature, whether for a paper or a major research project. Reading books, journals, and other material in the field allows one to become aware of the histories, contributing disciplines, and various issues of adult education. Graduate school is the one place where students have a responsibility to read broadly, to take time to examine what is out there, and to know how and what other students and authors have studied. As with any academic training, it is not always important to know exactly what has already been written, but it is important to know where to obtain such information. Time in the library is time well spent toward professional development. Chapters Two and Three in this volume provide further discussion of this topic.

**Dissertation and Thesis Writing.** Dissertations and master's theses can be considered both process and product. Hours and hours are spent researching, writing, thinking about, and breathing the study. Somehow these activities come together to form a written product that is the hallmark of a student's career, from which articles can later be written. Tackling a project of this magnitude at times brings on the loneliness of a long-distance runner. Writing is a lonely process, and in this instance, the finish line cannot be seen until the moment that the student hands in the final copy for binding. Like the runner, getting through the thesis or dissertation means taking one step at a time. While sticking to the goal is imperative, students need to take care of themselves through the process. This means creating a support group, learning to accept invitations from caring friends, and taking a day or weekend off now and then. Students traditionally are accorded the status of a nonperson, especially on their home campus, and it takes creativity and an eternal sense of optimism to move forward when funds are low, friends are far, and lofty thoughts are not forthcoming. Writing, thinking, and research skills are certainly sharpened while doing a study, and these skills, along with the exacting tasks of motivating, disciplining, and fighting fatigue, are all part of the professional development gained from writing a dissertation or thesis.

## Conclusion

Each of the activities described here contributes to the overall professional development of the student. This development occurs not all at once but slowly. As Buchanan (1987, p. 4) advises, "we don't become professional all at once. We advance toward it little by little, always leaning toward our development as a person. As you strive to improve yourself professionally and accomplish great things, you'll build character, strengthen self, and gain many rewards." Indeed, this has been my experience. My goals when entering graduate school were to take advantage of as many opportunities as I could along the way and, to the best of my ability, to enjoy the experience. I was fortunate to be in programs with supportive faculty that encouraged other students and me to engage in activities that promoted our development.

To a certain degree, all students can take advantage of some of the activities I have described, even if just on the local campus. If nothing else, graduate school can teach the intangibles for success in any career, such as perseverance, management of time and stress, collaboration, and interpersonal skills. Each student encounters different situations and choices, and each has a responsibility to seek out opportunities within his or her own environment. Working within one's own limits and circumstances may take some persistence and ingenuity, but it does pay off.

Slowly, over time, professional development does happen. What once seemed fuzzy to me ("I am not sure what I want to do . . . ") has evolved into clear, focused goals ("I want to take advantage of this opportunity because . . . "). Thinking through how graduate school can work in terms of strengthening competencies and the vita is a challenge but a rewarding one, and it ensures that the time spent pursuing an advanced degree is time devoted to the process of professional development.

## References

Brockett, R. G. "Professional Associations for Adult and Continuing Education." In S. B. Merriam and P. M. Cunningham (eds.), *Handbook of Adult and Continuing Education.* San Francisco: Jossey-Bass, 1989.

Brookfield, S. (ed.). *Training Educators of Adults: The Theory and Practice of Graduate Adult Education.* London and New York: Routledge, 1988.

Bruce, R., Maxwell, D., and Galvin, P. "Graduate Study and the Practice of Adult Education: A Problem of Congruence." *Lifelong Learning: An Omnibus of Practice and Research,* 1986, *10* (3), 4-7, 20.

Buchanan, P. J. "Much Ado About Professionalism." *Journal of Extension,* 1987, *25,* 3-4.

Commission of Professors of Adult Education. *Standards for Graduate Programs in Adult Education.* Washington, D.C.: American Association for Adult and Continuing Education, n.d.

Dowling, W. D., and Sheehan, V. J. "Benefits of Graduate Study in Adult Education for the Practitioner." *Lifelong Learning: The Adult Years,* 1982, *5* (9), 18-19.

Duke, C. "Training of Adult Educators." In C. J. Titmus (ed.), *Lifelong Education for Adults: An International Handbook.* Elmsford, N.Y.: Pergamon Press, 1989.

Fingeret, A. "Culture Shock: Practitioners Returning to Graduate School." *Lifelong Learning: The Adult Years,* 1983, *6* (10), 13-14.

Galbraith, M. W., and Zelenak, B. S. "The Education of Adult and Continuing Education Practitioners." In S. B. Merriam and P. M. Cunningham (eds.), *Handbook of Adult and Continuing Education.* San Francisco: Jossey-Bass, 1989.

Gschwender, E. "Graduate Programs in Education: Beyond Content to Professionalism." *Lifelong Learning: The Adult Years,* 1982, *6* (3), 15, 31.

Houle, C. O. "Professional Education for Educators of Adults." *Adult Education,* 1956, *6* (3), 131-141.

Lewis, L. H. "Coping with Change: Married Women in Graduate School." *Lifelong Learning: An Omnibus of Practice and Research,* 1983, *7* (1), 8-9, 28, 31.

Merriam, S. "Training Adult Educators in North America." *Convergence,* 1985, *18* (3-4), 84-93.

Pittman, V. "Some Things Practitioners Wish Adult Education Professors Would Teach." *Adult Learning,* 1989, *1* (3), 30.

Schuster, J. H., Wheeler, D. W., and Associates. *Enhancing Faculty Careers: Strategies for Development and Renewal.* San Francisco: Jossey-Bass, 1990.

Weaver, R. A., and Kowalski, T. J. "The Case for Program Accreditation of Doctoral Degrees in Adult Education." *Lifelong Learning: An Omnibus of Practice and Research,* 1987, *10* (7), 14-15, 26-27.

*Catherine P. Zeph is community adult education specialist with the University of Georgia Cooperative Extension Service. She received her master's in adult education from George Washington University and her doctorate in adult education from the University of Georgia.*

*Learning to practice reflectively can lead to improved professional and organizational effectiveness.*

# Strategies for Reflective Practice

*John M. Peters*

Work is not always challenging. It can be downright boring at times, even for professionals. Routine work or thoughtless work is meaningless. Since humans have a need for meaning in their lives, routine work can actually be harmful to one's health and well-being. Short of changing one's job, an antidote is to become a reflective practitioner.

Reflective practice is currently a popular topic of books and articles written for people interested in improving individual and organizational effectiveness. Reflective practice consists of "mindful consideration of one's actions" (Osterman, 1990, p. 134), in which the reasons and assumptions that drive one's behavior are thoughtfully reflected on in the interest of improving one's professional effectiveness. Thought and action are thus integrated through reflection. Osterman describes the process as a "challenging, focused, and critical assessment of one's behavior as a means toward the development of one's craftsmanship" (p. 134).

This chapter describes some ways in which the adult educator may become more reflective in practice. The bulk of the chapter describes and elaborates on a four-step approach to practicing reflectively.

## What Is Reflective Practice?

Reflective practice involves more than simply thinking about what one is doing and what one should do next. It involves identifying one's assumptions and feelings associated with practice, theorizing about how these assumptions and feelings are functionally or dysfunctionally associated with practice, and acting on the basis of the resulting theory of practice. In this sense, reflective practice involves critical thinking and learning, both of which are processes that can lead to significant self-development.

Reflective practice involves a kind of inquiry—indeed, a kind of research—that is not generally thought to be a component of work outside academic settings. As Schön (1983) puts it,

> When someone reflects-in-action, he becomes a researcher in the practice context. He is not dependent on the categories of established theory and technique, but constructs a new theory of the unique case. His inquiry is not limited to a deliberation about means which depends on a prior agreement about ends. He does not keep means and ends separate, but defines them interactively as he frames a problematic situation. He does not separate thinking from doing, ratiocinating his way to a decision which he must later convert to action. Because his experimenting is a kind of action, implementation is built into his inquiry [p. 68].

This means that the reflective practitioner is a student of his or her own actions and that the study of these actions is conducted in a systematic, analytical manner. A special kind of practice is involved—one that involves the practitioner in a sustained inquiry into the relationship between thought and action.

Reflective thinking also involves critical thinking, and this, according to Brookfield (1987), means "identifying and challenging assumptions and exploring and imagining alternatives" (p. 15). Such critical thinking is usually prompted by a surprise, a puzzlement, a confusion, or simply a recognition by the practitioner that his or her habitual ways of thinking and acting no longer result in effective practice. Sometimes critical thinking is prompted by "a discrepancy between the real and the ideal, or between what occurred and what was expected . . . [causing practitioners to] step back and examine their actions and the reasons for their actions" (Osterman, 1990, p. 134). Learning and professional growth usually occur when practitioners critically reflect and act on revised assumptions. Thus, not only is improved practice a desired result of reflective practice but professional development is as well.

## Steps to Reflective Practice

A person can learn, under the guidance of others or through self-direction, to be a reflective practitioner. This chapter emphasizes what practitioners may do for themselves in order to reflect in practice, even though they may occasionally involve others in their quest to be more reflective.

Learning to be more reflective in practice involves a kind of data collection; that is, it involves the assembling of information about oneself and the situation in which practice occurs. Analyzing these data can then lead to one or more theories about practice and the possibility of improvement. In fact, the term *data* suggests a handy acronym for conceptualizing the four steps to reflective practice:

1. Describe the problem, task, or incident that represents some critical aspect of practice needing examination and possible change.
2. Analyze the nature of what is described, including the assumptions that support the actions taken to solve the problem, task, or incident.
3. Theorize about alternative ways to approach the problem, task, or incident.
4. Act on the basis of the theory.

The remainder of the chapter describes how the practitioner may carry out these steps.

**Describe.** The first step of the DATA model involves a description of the problem, task, or incident on which the practitioner wishes to focus in order to improve his or her practice. (For the purpose of this discussion, the DATA steps will be explained in terms of solving a problem.) This step includes identifying and recounting the details of the problem and the actions taken to solve it. One should describe the problem and actions exactly as he or she sees them. The description should contain information about the setting in which the problem occurred, about other people involved, about events, and about the roles these people and the problem solver played in these events. The problem solver should also record his or her own thoughts and feelings related to each element of the description; however, the description should not include an interpretation or analysis of the problem and actions, for this will come later. The purpose of the first step is to put as much as possible "on the table" for later examination; thus, the more complete the description is, the better.

For an example of how this step might be carried out, consider the experience of a teacher of adults whom we will call "Charlie." Charlie has considerable experience in teaching children, but when he took a job in adult basic education, he decided to take a couple of graduate courses in the field to further his professional development. In his graduate study, Charlie learned that he and other adults learn best when they have some active role in planning and conducting their learning experiences. So he developed a plan for involving his adult students in designing their classroom work, and he promoted active discussion and dialogue around issues identified by students as important in their everyday lives. However, Charlie soon grew uncomfortable with the apparent lack of progress that his students were making toward their stated goals, and he gradually increased his own participation in the discussions, until finally he returned to a lecture-dominated technique of classroom instruction. He still believed that much more could be gained through experience-based discussion and dialogue, although he felt more comfortable lecturing. Thus, Charlie felt a tension between what he had come to believe about effective ways to facilitate adult learning and his own proclivity for the means of teaching most familiar to him. He wanted to improve his teaching, but he felt pressured by his own and his students' expectations that he stand up there and teach them something, and he did not know how to resolve this tension.

According to the DATA model, the first step Charlie should take is to describe his problem and his attempt to deal with it by identifying the context in which it occurred, the steps he took to implement his strategy of student involvement, the reactions of the students, and other aspects of the situation and events that took place. He should also describe the way he felt about his approach, about the students' reactions to it, and about his perceived need to abandon his first strategy in favor of a more conventional approach.

Several techniques may be helpful in completing this step. Two of the best sources for this purpose are Brookfield's (1987) *Developing Critical Thinkers* and Mezirow and Associates' (1990) *Fostering Critical Reflection in Adulthood*. In fact, these two books contain a number of techniques that are helpful at every step of the process described here.

One particularly worthwhile approach is to use the critical-incident technique, "which prompts [people] to identify an incident that for some reason was of particular significance to them" (Brookfield, 1987, p. 97). Using this technique, educators ask students to identify when and where the incident occurred, who were the people involved, and what made the incident critical to the person identifying it. The incident can involve some aspect of the workplace, or it can relate to the personal or social life of the problem solver. In any case, the description of the incident is used as a basis for analysis and discussion, usually by two or more people. For the purpose of the step being discussed here, the description need not be requested by another person or discussed with another.

Other sources that are useful for completing this step include those that describe phenomenological methods for collecting information about subjects of interest. These methods are used to describe a person's "life world" as it is understood by the person, not by an outside observer. For more on the phenomenological method, see Kvale (1983) and my own interpretation of the method (Peters, 1990). These sources describe how to interview others or observe them in action. However, one can apply phenomenological interviewing methods to "interviewing" oneself for the steps discussed here. In fact, it would be a good idea for the problem solver to tape-record this "interview" or at least to take copious notes as the description proceeds. This may seem awkward, but it works for some people. The remainder of the steps will be explained as if this approach is to be used.

**Analyze.** The analysis seeks to identify factors that contribute to the problem and to one's approach to solving it. Most problems faced in an area of practice such as adult education are "ill defined" (Hayes, 1978). This means that few problems have such clear parameters that everyone can agree on the problem definition and its solution, as people do on most math problems. In fact, one person may define similar problems quite differently from one case to the next. Thus, an important aspect of the analysis step is the identification of why the problem solver defined the problem in a particular way and the exploration of other possible interpretations. At this stage, the involvement of other people can be particularly helpful. When someone else reads or hears the problem description, he or she may interpret the problem differently than the problem solver does. At the least, another person can assist in a brainstorming procedure that seeks as many interpretations as possible; in some situations, the involvement of several other people may be productive.

Another level of the analysis involves understanding the reasons for one's own problem-solving actions. Returning to the description produced in step one, one should identify all of the actions taken and ask why each was taken. This analysis should also be recorded, and the statements themselves should then be subjected to analysis. One should listen for expressions of beliefs, rules, motives, and facts as he or she determines the reasons for the actions. One should then elaborate on each of these reasons, again recording these statements. Thus, as each reason is given, it, too, is analyzed, and the results of this analysis are analyzed, and so on, until one is pretty sure there is not much left to say. At this point, the recording is played back and examined for assumptions that the problem solver must have drawn on in order to take the actions identified. Finally, the assumptions themselves need to be examined in terms of their origin and appropriateness to the practice.

Our practitioner Charlie, for example, might sit back and think aloud, with or without a tape recorder, about the reasons he approached the classroom problem in the way described. He should also talk with others about the problem and his actions, sounding out his reasons and subjecting them to the scrutiny of others as well as to his own analysis. This dialogue should be free and open, with as few restraints and presuppositions as possible, and Charlie should be prepared to take a few jolts to his feelings. The objective of this exercise should be to bring to the surface beliefs and assumptions about teaching, learning, and the special role of experience and to subject these assumptions to further analysis. Such analysis is designed to identify and examine the sources of the assumptions and to speculate on their relevance to the type of work being done in the classroom. In Charlie's case, beliefs about teaching might have been formed by his own earlier experiences as a learner and by his training. However, while his earlier experiences might have left him with a model of teaching that is teacher-controlled and authoritarian in nature, his training might have exposed him to models that were learner-centered and democratic in nature. The latter might have proved more appealing to him as a teacher, but the former might have held sway over his decisions and actions, given the conditioning produced by his long exposure to that model. This combination of influences is almost certain to result in Charlie's ambivalence toward "proper" teaching methods and could help account for the frustration and change in strategy that were outlined in the problem description. These suppositions result from a preliminary analysis of the description, and they provide material for further analysis, such as an analysis of the relationship between Charlie's own experience as a learner and what he expects of learners under his guidance.

All levels of the analysis are intended to produce material for Charlie to use in reshaping his thinking about teaching and learning as they relate to the learner experience and to provide a basis for a revised personal theory about the way to deal with learner experience in the classroom.

Mezirow and Associates' (1990) book contains several chapters on techniques for helping others examine their assumptions with the aim of leading them to new perspectives on their life world. Such techniques include keeping a personal journal, writing an autobiography, using a repertory grid, and exploring the literature. Similarly, Chapter Seven in Brookfield (1987) is devoted to ideas for helping others examine assumptions underlying their thoughts and actions. Another excellent source of information on this topic is the February 1990 issue of the journal *Education and Urban Society* (see Osterman, 1990). This issue includes a discussion of techniques and examples from both teaching and administration, although most examples are drawn from childhood education. Finally, a recently published book by Schön (1991) is packed with examples of reflective practice.

**Theorize.** Scholars are not the only people who theorize. Practitioners also theorize, but not usually for the sake of theory itself. Indeed, we all theorize about what we do or ought to do, and this is a key element in understanding the way in which professionals practice. According to Argyris and Schön (1974), professionals have two kinds of theory in their repertoires: "espoused theories" and "theories in use." The former are what we draw on when asked to explain what we do, and the latter are the actual theories we employ when practicing. Sometimes these are in conflict with one another. Cervero (1988) elaborates on this distinction in a book on continuing education in the professions, a source that readers of this volume might find more relevant to their practice.

The analysis step is designed to sort out actual beliefs, rules, and motives that guide one's practice with respect to a particular problem. Through that step, the problem solver should have exposed much of his or her current theory about the actions involved. The result is not intended to be a formal theory in the scholarly sense, but it is enough to reveal how one thinks about what he or she does.

The third step involves taking the theory derived from the analysis step and developing it into a new one that promises to improve one's practice. The result should be material both for the problem solver's espoused theory and for his or her theory in action, since the goal is to make them the same.

In our example, Charlie might begin to theorize about how his own actions in the classroom affect the responses of his students. His theory might incorporate the particular effect that emotions play in such a situation. For example, let's say that his analysis brought to light his fear that "letting go of the reins" in the classroom would result in his own loss of control and that this would end in chaos and a possible loss of respect for Charlie from his students. On the other hand, he might also conclude that students bring their own fears to the classroom and that they, too, may resist exposing themselves and their experiences to others, including the teacher. He might then theorize that the experience-based strategy would be more successful if both his own fears and those of his students could be removed, and go on to speculate about ways in which this might be done. When his new theory is complete, Charlie is ready to test it by acting on it.

**Act.** Without action, all of the previous work remains theoretical, and not much changes. There are at least three reasons for taking action. First of all, the purpose of this whole effort is to improve practice. Second, action serves as a test of the theory developed in the third step. Third, the action itself can become the subject of further reflection and analysis. The process is thus like a spiral; each step offers an opportunity for reflection and a chance to return to earlier steps for deeper analysis.

In our example, Charlie would need to try out his theory about the role that fear plays in experiential learning, and he would want to study the outcome as it occurs. Critical reflection on the actions he takes to remove fear ought to result in a better understanding of his role as a teacher and of the way in which his beliefs and feelings influence his approach to teaching. Charlie thus assumes the role of researcher in his own classroom. With luck, this attitude will transfer to the students themselves, making them his collaborators in the process.

## Conclusion

Reflective practice is a special kind of practice. It involves a systematic inquiry into the practice itself, even as the practice is under way. It also requires that the practitioner be open to a scrutiny of beliefs, values, and feelings that may be strongly held and about which there is great sensitivity. Thus, reflective practice is not always pleasant, but it is almost always rewarding. Professional development is one reward, and better service to others is another.

## References

Argyris, C., and Schön, D. A. *Theory in Practice: Increasing Professional Effectiveness.* San Francisco: Jossey-Bass, 1974.

Brookfield, S. D. *Developing Critical Thinkers: Challenging Adults to Explore Alternative Ways of Thinking and Acting.* San Francisco: Jossey-Bass, 1987.

Cervero, R. M. *Effective Continuing Education for Professionals.* San Francisco: Jossey-Bass, 1988.

Hayes, J. R. *Cognitive Psychology: Thinking and Creating.* Belmont, Calif.: Dorsey Press, 1978.

Kvale, S. "The Qualitative Research Interview: A Phenomenological and Hermeneutical Mode of Understanding." *Journal of Phenomenological Psychology,* 1983, 14 (1), 171–196.

Mezirow, J., and Associates. *Fostering Critical Reflection in Adulthood: A Guide to Transformative and Emancipatory Learning.* San Francisco: Jossey-Bass, 1990.

Osterman, K. F. "Reflective Practice: A New Agenda for Education." *Education and Urban Society,* 1990, 22 (2), 133–152.

Peters, J. M. "The Action-Reason-Thematic Technique: Spying on the Self." In J. Mezirow and Associates, *Fostering Critical Reflection in Adulthood: A Guide to Transformative and Emancipatory Learning.* San Francisco: Jossey-Bass, 1990.

Schön, D. A. *The Reflective Practitioner.* New York: Basic Books, 1983.

Schön, D. A. (ed.). *The Reflective Turn.* New York: Teachers College Press, 1991.

*John M. Peters is professor of adult education and coordinator of the graduate program in adult education at the University of Tennessee, Knoxville.*

*A professional development plan involves turning ideas into action.*

# Planning for Professional Development

*Ralph G. Brockett*

Professional development can take many forms. The ideas presented in the previous chapters are intended to stimulate thinking about the range of possibilities for educators of adults who wish to embrace new professional growth opportunities. But these are merely ideas, and they must be translated into action to have a real impact.

So, then, how do we get from idea to action? This chapter suggests using a planning process that involves an active, conscious effort to incorporate professional development activities into the repertoire of daily practice. The chapter first provides some thoughts on ways to articulate a personal development plan. Second, it identifies major themes gleaned from the previous chapters that can be used in implementing such a plan.

## Articulating a Professional Development Plan

The concept of planning is crucial to successful professional development. Planning is intended to facilitate the achievement of some desired future outcome. In other words, by making decisions now about how we envision ourselves practicing as educators of adults and by taking active steps toward achieving that vision, we can create new opportunities for professional and personal success.

This chapter cannot provide an extensive discussion of different planning models. There are many books that discuss the planning of adult and continuing education activities, at both the program and instructional levels, and these apply to adult educators' own planning of their professional development. Some examples of excellent program-planning resources include books by Houle (1972), Knowles (1980), and Simerly and Associates

NEW DIRECTIONS FOR ADULT AND CONTINUING EDUCATION, no. 51, Fall 1991 © Jossey-Bass Inc., Publishers

(1987); resources emphasizing teaching and learning aspects of planning include Brookfield (1986), Knox (1986), and Hiemstra and Sisco (1990). The important point is that professional development is much too important to leave to chance and that every educator of adults should develop and articulate a professional development plan. Some may wish to accomplish this through a formal process replete with clear objectives, implementation strategies, evaluation procedures, and target dates. Others may prefer something a bit less structured. The important point is this: if one does not take the time to develop some sort of conscious plan that makes professional development an ongoing priority, such efforts are likely to become lost in the day-to-day routine of practice.

Stubblefield's (1981) four-phase learning-project model provides a simple yet comprehensive framework that can be used in articulating a professional development plan. Each of its phases is discussed briefly here.

**Initiating.** During this phase, one establishes a rationale for the learning project (or plan). This might include assessing professional goals and desired directions. Here one determines strengths, areas for improvement, and time frames for accomplishing specific goals.

**Planning.** According to Stubblefield, this phase consists of three steps: identifying available resources, determining activities that will lead to achieving one's purposes, and setting criteria for completing the project. Depending on the planning model one wishes to use, these three general steps can be further broken down into more detailed steps.

**Managing.** This is essentially the action phase of the process, where the plan is put into motion. The three steps in this phase, according to Stubblefield (1981) are "(1) completing each activity, (2) organizing and interpreting the data generated by the activities, and (3) recording progress toward changing an attitude, acquiring a skill, producing a product, or reporting findings about a topic" (p. 25).

**Evaluating.** This final phase stresses the extent to which purposes have been achieved. Evaluation should not be thought of in the black-and-white terms of *success* or *failure*. Instead, one can at this stage assess the extent to which initial objectives have been met, reassess priorities, and refocus directions for future efforts. Evaluation should be viewed as an ongoing process rather than merely as an exercise that emphasizes outcomes.

## Some Themes in Professional Development Planning

The previous nine chapters look at professional development from different angles. Taken together, however, the chapters address several themes that can serve as a basis for decisions about the directions to pursue in one's professional development. Thus, to close this volume, I would like to address four interrelated themes: the importance of self-awareness, the value of the professional literature as a tool for practice, the link between professional development and making contributions to the profession, and the importance of taking a proactive approach to one's professional development.

**Self-Awareness.** One of the most important points stressed throughout this volume is that self-awareness is crucial to successful professional development. Understanding such elements as one's basic value system, strengths, limitations, and aspirations provides the basis for planning. It is through self-awareness that each of us has the potential to forge a vision for the future. In the first chapter, the discussion of professional style centers on the notion that each of us is unique and that this uniqueness is one of our greatest resources. Indeed, style is something that emerges as one becomes aware of these unique qualities and builds on them. Similarly, the concept of reflective practice, addressed by Peters in Chapter Nine, is based on the assumption that critical reflection, which involves self-awareness, allows one to be transformed.

**Importance of the Professional Literature.** A second theme, central to the chapters by Imel, Stubblefield, and Hayes, is that the literature of adult and continuing education is an invaluable tool for professional development. Our field has a rich heritage, and much of this heritage has been documented through books, monographs, reports, and periodicals. Many of these publications are easily accessed through data bases, such as that maintained by the Educational Resources Information Center (ERIC), and through interlibrary loan policies. When examining the literature of adult and continuing education, we should look at both contemporary and historical sources. Contemporary sources may provide a cutting-edge perspective on the field, but the historical literature can be at least as valuable since it offers perspectives that have stood the test of time and provides a sense of how the field has evolved.

Since the 1970s, adult and continuing education research has mushroomed both in quantity and quality. Yet many educators tend to shy away from the research-based literature, often because they believe they do not understand research methods. Chapter Four in this volume offers the basic understanding necessary to negotiate some of the terminology and data analysis procedures used in most research studies.

**Making a Contribution to the Professional Community.** Successful professional development is a give-and-take proposition. In other words, viewing this activity as a one-way transmission of information limits possibilities for growth. Professional development, at its most effective, is actually an exchange among professionals. Thus, an important aspect of development is the ability to share one's ideas and insights with others. The chapters by Fulton, Dominick, and Shelton and Spikes address three vehicles through which individuals can engage in professional sharing. Activities such as writing for publication, making presentations, and taking leadership roles in professional associations are frequently associated with the academic side of the field. However, as adult and continuing education strives to play a more influential role in our society, we will need to create new networks in the field. This means that practitioners and academicians will need to find more direct ways to engage with one another. And it also means that educators from the many diverse interest areas that make up our field will need to search for the common ground that unites us all. This can only be achieved if we are willing to share our insights and ideas with colleagues across the field.

**A Proactive Approach.** A fourth theme, one that undergirds each of the previous chapters, is that successful professional development is most likely to occur when one takes a proactive approach to the process. When practitioners think of professional development as merely keeping up with the rapid changes that are taking place in the field, they are taking a reactive approach to their practice and professional development. On the other hand, the individual who views professional development as a basic responsibility is in a much stronger position to make decisions about the nature, substance, and process of these efforts.

In a recent discussion of self-direction in adult learning, Brockett and Hiemstra (1991) suggest that self-direction is dependent on one's taking personal responsibility for one's learning. In the previous chapters, some of the ideas clearly lend themselves to this notion of proactivity. The three chapters on contributing to the field all stress the importance of taking action. And the chapter by Peters is clearly grounded in the process of taking action that is based on critical reflection. But other chapters that may at first seem passive, also support the notion of active self-direction. For instance, some might think of reading as a passive activity; however, when one takes a proactive approach to reading, literature can take on new life and applicability. Knowles (1975) has offered some tips that can be used in this process of reading proactively.

Another example that may initially seem to be a passive approach to professional development is graduate study. However, as Zeph points out in Chapter Eight, the graduate experience consists of more than classes, papers, exams, and thesis or dissertation; the person who enters the graduate program with a definite agenda can get much more from the experience. It is when graduate study is approached in a proactive way that it can truly become a vehicle for professional development.

## Conclusion

Adult and continuing education has come a long way over the past century. As we look to the year 2000, the potential of the field is virtually unlimited. Yet it continues to face many struggles. It would be naive to think that if every person practicing in the field would simply engage in the strategies proposed in this book, these problems would cease to exist. But until adult and continuing educators gain a greater sense of their professional identity and of the kinds of directions they would like to see the field take in the coming years and until they take action to secure these directions, we run the risk of stagnation. What we do, as educators of adults, is simply much too important to allow that to happen. Let's make the future work to the benefit of those whom we serve by making our own growth and development an integral part of what we do.

## References

Brockett, R. G., and Hiemstra, R. *Self-Direction in Adult Learning: Perspectives on Theory, Research, and Practice.* London and New York: Routledge, 1991.

Brookfield, S. D. *Understanding and Facilitating Adult Learning: A Comprehensive Analysis of Principles and Effective Practices.* San Francisco: Jossey-Bass, 1986.

Hiemstra, R., and Sisco, B. *Individualizing Instruction: Making Learning Personal, Empowering, and Successful.* San Francisco: Jossey-Bass, 1990.

Houle, C. O. *The Design of Education.* San Francisco: Jossey-Bass, 1972.

Knowles, M. S. *Self-Directed Learning: A Guide for Learners and Teachers.* Englewood Cliffs, N.J.: Cambridge, 1975.

Knowles, M. S. *The Modern Practice of Adult Education: From Pedagogy to Andragogy.* (Rev. and updated ed.) Englewood Cliffs, N.J.: Cambridge, 1980.

Knox, A. B. *Helping Adults Learn: A Guide to Planning, Implementing, and Conducting Programs.* San Francisco: Jossey-Bass, 1986.

Simerly, R. G., and Associates. *Strategic Planning and Leadership in Continuing Education: Enhancing Organizational Vitality, Responsiveness, and Identity.* San Francisco: Jossey-Bass, 1987.

Stubblefield, H. W. "A Learning Project Model for Adults." *Lifelong Learning: The Adult Years,* 1981, 4 (7), 24–26.

*Ralph G. Brockett is associate professor of adult education at the University of Tennessee, Knoxville.*

# INDEX

AAACE. *See* American Association for Adult and Continuing Education

AAEA. *See* American Association for Adult Education

AARP. *See* American Association of Retired Persons

ABI/Inform, 19

Action research: defined, 38

Addams, J., 29, 33

Adler, M. J., 30, 33

Adrian, J. G., 56, 58

Adult and continuing education: commitment to, 10-11; and contributions to the community, 99-100; historical perspective of, 6; image problem of, 15; personal philosophy of, 10; professional associations in, 72-73; traditional education *vs.*, 6-7

Adult and Continuing Education Research Collection (Syracuse University), 17-18

*Adult Development and Learning,* 27

Adult Education Association of the United States (AEA/USA), 72

Adult Education Network (AEDNET), 21

*Adult Education Quarterly,* 16, 32

Adult Education Research Conference, 83-84

*Adult Education State Resource and Information Centers,* 20

*Adult Learning,* 16, 32, 52, 80

Adult Learning and Literacy Clearinghouse, 20, 23

*Adult Learning: Research and Practice,* 26

Adult Performance Level test, 36-37

AEA/USA. *See* Adult Education Association of the United States

AEDNET. *See* Adult Education Network

AgeLine, 19

American Association for Adult and Continuing Education (AAACE), 32, 55, 72-73, 77, 83-84

American Association for Adult Education (AAAE), 42, 72

American Association of Retired Persons (AARP), 19

American Society for Training and Development (ASTD), 32, 55, 72, 84

Applied research: defined, 37-38

*Applied Sociology,* 30

Apps, J. W., 10, 12, 51, 58

Argyris, C., 94, 96

Artistry: in professional development, 8-9

Aslanian, C. B., 40, 46

Association for Continuing Higher Education, 84

ASTD. *See* American Society for Training and Development

Atchity, K. J., 50, 53, 58

Audience: analysis of, for public presentations, 65-66

Barrows, H. S., 22, 23

Basic research: defined, 37

Beard, C. A., 6

Becker, H. S., 15, 23, 50, 53-55, 58

BEI. *See* British Education Index

Belenky, M. F., 27, 33

Belsheim, D. J., 41, 46

Bennis, W., 1, 3, 12

Berkowitz, R. E., 23

BITNET, 56

Blair, K. J., 27, 33

Books: as resource for professional development, 16

Boone, E. J., 27, 33

Borg, W. R., 42, 46

Boshier, R., 40, 46

Bovee, C. L., 61, 69, 70

Brickell, H. M., 40, 46

British Education Index (BEI), 19

Brockett, R. G., 28, 32, 33, 72-73, 78, 83, 88, 100, 101

Brookfield, S. D., 28, 33, 80, 88, 90, 92, 94, 96, 97-98, 101

*BRS Information Technologies 1990 Database Catalog,* 18, 23

Bruce, R., 80, 88

Bryson, L., 6, 30, 33

Buchanan, P. J., 87, 88

Budgeting: and skills gained in professional associations, 74

Canadian Association for the Study of Adult Education, 55-56

# ORDERING INFORMATION

NEW DIRECTIONS FOR ADULT AND CONTINUING EDUCATION is a series of paperback books that explores issues of common interest to instructors, administrators, counselors, and policy makers in a broad range of adult and continuing education settings—such as colleges and universities, extension programs, businesses, the military, prisons, libraries, and museums. Books in the series are published quarterly in fall, winter, spring, and summer and are available for purchase by subscription as well as by single copy.

SUBSCRIPTIONS for 1991 cost $45.00 for individuals (a savings of 20 percent over single-copy prices) and $60.00 for institutions, agencies, and libraries. Please do not send institutional checks for personal subscriptions. Standing orders are accepted.

SINGLE COPIES cost $13.95 when payment accompanies order. (California, New Jersey, New York, and Washington, D.C., residents please include appropriate sales tax.) Billed orders will be charged postage and handling.

DISCOUNTS FOR QUANTITY ORDERS are available. Please write to the address below for information.

ALL ORDERS must include either the name of an individual or an official purchase order number. Please submit your order as follows:
*Subscriptions:* specify series and year subscription is to begin
*Single copies:* include individual title code (such as CE1)

MAIL ALL ORDERS TO:
Jossey-Bass Inc., Publishers
350 Sansome Street
San Francisco, California 94104

FOR SALES OUTSIDE OF THE UNITED STATES CONTACT:
Maxwell Macmillan International Publishing Group
866 Third Avenue
New York, New York 10022

OTHER TITLES AVAILABLE IN THE
NEW DIRECTIONS FOR ADULT AND CONTINUING EDUCATION SERIES
*Ralph G. Brockett*, Editor-in-Chief
*Alan B. Knox*, Consulting Editor